31 Blessons:

Developing Your Own Recipes for Success

Christen Miller

31 Blessons: Developing Your Own Recipes for Success

Copyright © 2019 by Christen Miller

All rights reserved. No part of this book may be reproduced or transmitted in any form or by any means without written permission from the author.

ISBN: 978-0-578-22608-8

Printed in USA by 48HrBooks
(http://www.48HrBooks.com)

DEDICATION

First and foremost, I give God all of the honor and praise. Thank You for choosing and using me as a vessel to display to others on how You have worked in my life even through my darkest days.

To my parents, Christopher and Rumiko Miller, thank you for supporting, grounding and nurturing me with the drive and motivation to succeed at anything that I set my mind to do.

To my sisters, La'Donya Benning and Tamiko Miller, thank you for encouraging me to write this book and to step out of my comfort zone.

To my God Parents, Wayne and Tammie Staton, thank you for believing in me when there were days that I did not believe in myself.

To my best friends that have become family, Mykeia Clay, Tenisha Dunlap, Lacretia Harvey, Yadira Amerson, Marissa Palmer, Tabitha Wilson, Samod Wilson, and Jamerus Payton, thank you for ALWAYS being a true friend.

To my partner and dear friend, Dr. Jalaal Hayes, thank you for being a mentor, motivator, coach, and praying partner in preparation for this journey.

To Ms. Phyllis Sneed, thank you for trailblazing the entrepreneur journey for me.

To Mrs. Bonny Valentine, thank you for your prayers and continuous words of encouragement.

To each person that this book reaches globally, thank you for allowing me to aspire to inspire you. Understand that each of your lessons in life serve as a greater purpose for you and the world. In hard times, do not be discouraged or dismayed because God is directly on your side. Application is the key to your success, so be sure to surround yourself with great people and become MIA (Motivated, Innovated, Activated) in all that you do.

I love you all.

Contents

Introduction 8

Chapter 1 10

Blessons: Life Vs. Death 10

Chapter 2 11

Blessons: Growing Up Military 11

Chapter 3 15

Blessons: Trials & Tribulations Part 1 15

Chapter: 4 19

Blessons: Trials And Tribulations Part 2 .. 19

Chapter 5 23

Blessons: Move Pt. 1 23

Chapter 6 26

Blessons: Move Pt. 2 26

Chapter 7 30

Blessons: Move Pt. 3 30

Chapter 8 34

Blessons: Entrepreneur Like And Follow 34

Chapter 9 37

Blessons: Caught In The Hype Of Entrepreneurship ... 37

Chapter 10 42

Blessons: Entrepreneur Set Your Price And Be Quiet .. 42

Chapter: 11 45
Blessons: Qualified By Purpose 45
Chapter 12 49
Blessons: Experience Is The Best Key 49
Chapter: 13 52
Blessons: Beauty In Brokenness 52
Chapter 14 56
Blessons: The Masked Runner 56
Chapter 15 60
Blessons: Pass Or Fail 60
Chapter16 64
Blessons: The Power In Healing 64
Chapter 17 68
Blessons: The Day I Married Myself 68
Chapter 18 71
Blessons: Out With The Old 71
Chapter 19 77
Blessons: Spiritual Food 77
Chapter 20 81
Blessons: Happiness & Joy 81
Chapter 21 84
Blessons: All By Myself 84
Chapter: 22 88

Blessons: Social Comparison 88

Chapter: 23 92

Blessons: Peace Within The Fight 92

Chapter: 24 96

Blessons: Push Season 96

Chapter 25 100

Blessons: Faith Test 100

Chapter 26 103

Blessons: Process Of Purpose 103

Chapter 27 107

Blessons: Self Talk 107

Chapter 28 111

Blessons: Are You Grateful? 111

Chapter 29 115

Blessons: Dark Places 115

Chapter 30 119

Blessons: Trust 119

Chapter 31 123

Blessons: Birthing 123

About The Author 128

Blessons Business Sponsors 129

Counseling Hotlines 134

References 138

Introduction

Behind each successful smile, there will be at least one person that will be real and say "Although I Smile, You Don't Know My Story."

It is hard to overcome our toughest battles when we think we have to be strong all of the time, make sense of every component of our lives, or even place control measures on what happens next. Growing up in a "microwaveable generation" can be quite confusing when we leave out the ingredients in the process, but little do we know is the ingredients used in the process is what helps develop recipes to reach our progress.

The purpose for this book is to gain understanding that anything worth having, writing about, or lasting for a lifetime will take time, blood, sweat, and a few tears. You will go through trials and tribulations and have to make major sacrifices, but it is through your perspective on how you view your trials. Will you view them as burdens or as lessons to blessings?

Just imagine yourself as a rubber band being stretched to the capacity with trying to live your best life, finances, relationships, business, family, friends, school, and then all of a sudden you wake up one morning and it feels like you want to scream and the sound of your rubber band goes POP!!!

If this is you, take a deep breath and allow me to reassure you that your rubber band has reinforced to pull you back to its normal state. You have been saved by God's grace in reaching new heights and endeavors in what is called the stretching season. You may not understand and many people may not agree, but if you continue to have faith, you will surely make a way out of no way.

Through this book, you will learn that it was through my life lessons that gave me the recipes to follow and connect with my greater blessings. It is through your process, I pray you will connect with God so that He can help motivate, innovate, and activate the purpose and promise that He has within you. I believe in you and you should too.

IT IS TIME TO GET YOUR BLESSONS!!!

"I know the plans that I have for you says the Lord, they are for good and not for evil, designed for a hope and future" (Jeremiah 29:11 NLT)

Chapter 1
Blessons: Life vs. Death

"**Congratulations!!!** You're having a baby," are the words that someone once said to your mother while you were developing in her womb. Even before you were formed within your mother's womb, God knew who you were and the overall purpose that He had upon your life.

Nine long months and then one day your mother's water breaks and now she is rushed to the hospital preparing to bring you into this world at any moment. In much exhaust, pain, and labor for 12.5 hours, your mother gives one last hard push and you enter the world of the unknown, but something is not quite right.

You enter the world black and blue due to an umbilical cord wrapped around your throat. Once you grasped the attention of your doctor, they perform very quickly to save you, clean you up, and place you in the arms of a loved one.

With only a couple of bruises, you open your eyes, take your first breath and realize you SURVIVED. Who was this child that lived and not died? Me. Welcome to the beginning of my 31 Blessons.

"I knew you before I formed you in your mother's womb. Before you were born, I set you apart and appointed you as my prophet to the nations." (Jeremiah 1:5 NLT).

Chapter 2
Blessons: Growing Up Military

As a child, I grew up with more adults than I did children and was far more advanced in life than most my age. The majority of my time was spent with my grandparents and uncle as both my mother and father worked to provide for me. Once my father enlisted into the military, my whole life changed and now it would just be my mother, father, and I traveling to different countries.

At the age of five, I could remember attending at least four different schools for kindergarten all in the same year. We were stationed in one place to only receive orders to move to another. Imagine how that would have felt at the age of five trying to establish friendships? It was somewhat of a challenge, but one thing I learned to do was to adapt to change. Being a "Military Brat" taught me different cultures, togetherness, but of all to enjoy the moment because at any time we could move.

Our last duty station was in Hawaii where I stayed until the fourth grade and then it was back home to North Carolina to be closer to family. Adjusting became the new normal, but when coming back to North Carolina, I had a hard time in elementary school because the learning pace for students was much faster than it was in Hawaii; therefore, I really devoted a lot of my time to my studies.

Entering middle school was a new journey for me. The excitement of exceling in academics, making friends, and joining organizations that I was interested in allowed me to develop an identity of my own. I was physically active in sports, spiritually active within my church community, and overall seemed mentally and emotionally well until September 11, 2001. This would be the day that I would realize what it really meant to be a Military Brat.

At a young age, this was one of the scariest moments of my life. Not only was I distraught about witnessing the second plane crashing into the second tower, but to know that my dad was going to war because of this, saddened me deeply. I did not know what to expect, how to say goodbye, and of all I kept asking myself: *Was he going to be safe and return?* All of these things were racing through my mind at the age of 13.

As a Military Brat, you learn to be accustomed to your parent going to trainings or weeks in the field, but not for war. With my dad being deployed, it taught me a sense of responsibility, strength, and also that I could never be weak because my job was to help my mom take care of my sisters as she was now technically a single parent. After my dad returned back from war, I was overjoyed, but then about a couple of years later came a new duty station for him to report. At this point of my life I was sick of moving and meeting new friends and I became normalized to my mother raising my sisters and I as a single parent. No this was not my father's choice, but in order to provide us with the things we needed, he had to do it.

Due to the circumstances, I began adulting at a very young age. Working my first job at the age of 16 with a car of my own, taking care of the maintenance of the car, paying my own phone bill, helping to raise my two sisters while attending school all served as the introduction to my adult life. My mom did a great job being present at each one of our softball games, band performances, award ceremonies, and so much more to fulfill the gap of my dad not being there, but there were other times when my dad would drive 10 hours to surprise us at our games when he had the opportunity to do so. Those were the days that really warmed my heart.

Closer to graduating from high school is when I would realize even though my mother did the best that she could and my father did what he had to do, I would finally begin to process how the life of the military took a toll on me. A decision I knew not made to hurt me, but to provide me with a better life, affected me emotionally. For years, my dad was pulled away on different assignments and duties, but I know that if he could have been present every moment, he would. This was my true experience of what it is was like being a Military Brat.

"Don't be afraid, for I am with you. Don't be discouraged, for I am your God. I will strengthen you and help you. I will hold you up with my victorious right hand."
(Isaiah 41:10 NLT)

- **Lesson:** It is not always easy when it comes to sacrificing.
- **Blessing:** Through the many tours in the military, my dad always returned back home safely.
- **Recipe:** Allow yourself to seek wise counsel when you feel that you are not emotionally healthy.

~JOURNAL MY BLESSON~

Think of a time in your life when you felt emotionally challenged. What happened? What did you learn? How did your lesson serve as a blessing later in life? What recipe can you develop to help you move forward?

- ❖ Situation:

- ❖ Lesson:

- ❖ Blessing:

- ❖ Recipe:

Chapter 3

Blessons: Trials & Tribulations Part 1

Over the years of gaining much wisdom and knowledge, I find myself still learning that the test of your patience and building of your endurance lie within trials and tribulations. Time periods of going through distress, persecution, or just even a trying experience can seem overwhelming but overall, the beauty is discovering how to overcome the process.

Devoting my life back to Christ was a major step that I made in 2011. With the assumption of doing right everything was supposed to go right; however, I was wrong. The implementation of many changes allowed me to have high expectations for the following year, but little did I know that this would be one of the worst years of my life.

The year 2012, was very exciting for me. I began a new faith walk and enrolled into my first class in graduate school while also preparing for a career in the military. Life was great until my 24th birthday. As always, I was shown love on this day by text, phone calls, and overwhelming posts on social media that shared happy birthday, but I never knew how I would value the last words of a friend that I would never see again.

Responding back to all of my posts to each person that evening, I specifically remember one late post from my dearest friend that I met during my freshman year in college. He posted on my wall happy birthday and we conversed back and forth for a little while. His final words were to enjoy the rest of my day and that we would catch up and go shopping soon.

That evening my friends and I went out of town for dinner. We laughed, ate, took pictures, and overall made everlasting memories. We traveled back home that night stuck in traffic, getting in a little after midnight. Each of us prepared for bed as we all had to wake up for church the next morning. In a deep sleep, my phone rang and the call was from my best friend's brother. He sounded as if something was wrong, but I was so exhausted that I could not make out any words that he was saying other than to call him back when I awoke.

As I hung up the phone and went back to sleep, I replayed that phone conversation in my mind and by the sound of my friend's brother's voice I knew something was not right, so I called him back. I called him back to only hear that my friend that I just had a conversation with hours ago wishing me a happy birthday had been murdered in the early hours of the next morning. In shock, I quickly denied the information and searched social media to see any recent post but there was no news at all; so therefore, I felt that everything was alright and went back to sleep. The next morning, I woke up and checked social media again to only see a timeline of posts that said RIP, talk about devastated and traumatized! How could someone you just spoke to be gone in a matter of hours? Who would do something like this? Why was he murdered? What about his family? These were all the questions that were going through my mind as I was sitting in disbelief.

I called my college friend to see if she was okay as this was her child's father that had been murdered, but I could not get in contact with her. It was about three weeks later that we were able to speak to one another for the first time since the tragedy. Losing a dear friend to gun violence hurt me, but I could not even position myself of how it would forever affect my college friend losing her child's father. When I spoke to her, I did not ask any questions; however, I did state I was available at any time that she needed me. I explained to her that we would get through this process together, and it was in that moment where our bond became stronger than college friends, we then became spiritual sisters.

"Two people are better off than one, for they can help each other succeed. If one person falls, the other can reach out and help. But someone who falls alone is in real trouble." (Ecclesiastes 4:9-10 NLT)

- **Lesson**: Every day is not promised so enjoy every moment you have with your loved ones.
- **Blessing**: I was able to speak to my dear friend one last time and also gained a spiritual sister.
- **Recipe**: Although you may go through hard times be able to display true empathy for others in their hard times.

~JOURNAL MY BLESSON~

Think of a time in your life when you had to empathize with someone, what happened? What did you learn? How did your lesson serve as a blessing later in life? What recipe can you develop to help you move forward?

- ❖ Situation:

- ❖ Lesson:

- ❖ Blessing:

- ❖ Recipe:

Chapter: 4

Blessons: Trials and Tribulations Part 2

After developing my own way of coping with the loss of my dear friend, I returned back to my routine with working full-time, being available for my new spiritual sister as she needed me, taking my first graduate class, and preparing myself to begin my process for the military, but little did I know I would be hit with the devastating news of my dad being diagnosed with cancer. It had only been five months after my friends' death and now I was hit with this! That day, I questioned my new faith walk. It was very often that I thought about how I was trying to do everything right, but everything I was facing throughout the year seemed as if I were being punished for doing wrong.

When my parents sat both my sister and I down to tell us about his new cancer diagnosis, we were confused. Cancer never ran through our family, nobody has ever been sick, and we really did not experience death with our family members. It was a point in time where I believed that I was really blessed to say I had two living grandmothers and most people could not. My family lived, and were healthy people for life, were my thoughts. Once my parents explained to us what we needed to hear, I asked to be excused and left out of the house in rage, slamming the door behind me. *Why is this happening to me? What did I do to deserve this? Will my dad be able to walk me down the aisle for my wedding day?* These were all the questions I was asking as I sat by myself in my car.

Not knowing who to turn to in the midst of a life changing moment, I called my new spiritual sister and she was in the transitioning time of slowly piecing her life back together. We had become close over a time period, but who would have ever known that the tables would turn where I would need her the most. As I sat in my car, I called her and cried. She asked me repeatedly what was wrong, and then she just stopped and allowed me to have my moment. Finally mustering up enough strength to tell her that my dad had cancer, she quickly went into spiritual sister mode with first praying but to tell the truth, prayer was not the first thing on my list to do after receiving news of such. She then explained that whatever I needed she would be there and then suddenly it dawned on me, where she gave me my own words back saying that, "We will get through this together."

Knowing that I had at least one person that would be present for me and was able to empathize meant the world even through the hurt. This was the day my life changed, I no longer was interested in joining the military and I knew I had to regain focus in school, but once again realizing that life was too short to be taken advantage of because at any moment things could change.

"So then, since Christ suffered physical pain, you must arm yourselves with the same attitude he had, and be ready to suffer, too. For if you have suffered physically for Christ, you have finished with sin." (1 Peter 4:1 NLT)

- **Lesson**: Making a commitment to serve on a greater level does not leave you exempt from trials nor tribulations.
- **Blessing**: I had a spiritual sister in the process of my pain.

- **Recipe:** Be sure that you have a friend that can pray for you in times that you cannot pray for yourself.

~JOURNAL MY BLESSON~

Think of a time in your life when someone had to help you with the process of healing, what happened? What did you learn? How did your lesson serve as a blessing later in life? What recipe can you develop to help you move forward?

- ❖ Situation:

- ❖ Lesson:

- ❖ Blessing:

- ❖ Recipe:

Chapter 5

Blessons: Move Pt. 1

Has there ever been a time where you were in the way of someone and they told you to move? More than likely you probably got out of the way so that there would be no problems. Could you ever imagine moving out the way of your fear, comfort, or anxiety? Would you be able to move?

As I began working at the credit union, I seemed to have become complacent working a 9-5 job because I did not have to work weekends nor holidays as I did when I worked in the retail industry; increased pay and benefits also registered as a plus. Although I felt as such, there was something on the inside of me that knew that there was more to life then benefits, holiday pay, and counting thousands of dollars daily to people that I did not make myself. The thought of moving to do something greater was always in me, but there was so much anxiety and fear of exactly what to do.

One day at work, I sat on the teller line and heard the word MOVE! I constantly questioned what move really meant and what it looked like, as I knew it was pertaining to my job. At the time, I was enrolled into my first Master's program focusing on Marriage and Family Counseling. Therefore, I automatically thought I was supposed to find a job in relation to my field of study because it only made sense to me. Operating in obedience, I began searching for positions closely related to my major, and after being denied so many times, I just quit.

The year 2014 came and I knew that I was going to have a great year, because this was the year that I would obtain my Master's Degree. Working full time, paying my bills, maintaining a 3.5 GPA, and mentoring a young lady allowed me to be content with life, but it was in March of 2014 when I heard God tell me to start a youth program. One fact about me is that working with the youth to help them succeed serves as a passion in my life, so the idea of it was great, but my question was: *Where did I begin?*

Frustrated with trying to put everything together, I developed an attitude and I remember praying in my bedroom that night that if I was supposed to start something, then I would be given a business name. Once I finished my prayers and got into bed, I heard the word F.E.L.P and was in shock to hear an answer so quickly, but I also developed another attitude because the name F.E.L.P just did not sound like a business name. So once again I asked for clarification of what the acronym F.E.L.P stood for? The next morning when I woke up, I knew what the acronym F.E.L.P stood for, Future Endeavors Life Program, and my first participant in the program was the young lady that I was mentoring already. This was my next major move.

"Your word is a lamp to guide my feet and a light for my path." (Psalms 119:105 NLT)

- **My Lesson:** Never become complacent in life.
- **My Blessing:** I was given the opportunity to birth a program **that** would aspire youth.
- **My Recipe:** Learn to listen to your inner self.

~JOURNAL MY BLESSON~

Think of a time when you had to make a big move, what happened? What did you learn? How did your lesson serve as a blessing later in life? What recipe can you develop to help you move forward?

- ❖ Situation:

- ❖ Lesson:

- ❖ Blessing:

- ❖ Recipe:

Chapter 6

Blessons: Move Pt. 2

After seeing the vision and allowing it to be made plain, I began utilizing my school and community resources. I never owned a business or much less started anything ever, but I knew that it was time, and in the process that I would educate myself. I continued to mentor the young lady that I had previous through another program and enrolled her into F.E.L.P. Her heart was filled with joy because she had the opportunity to be a part of something that would enhance her abilities as she grew older in life.

It was very ironic to speak to my spiritual sister about everything new that was occurring in my life because she too was beginning a new program called Nariah's Way Foundation. The mission of her organization would serve grieving children that have lost a parent to gun violence. This program was not only going to help children, but it was also going to help my spiritual sister as she was learning to cope with the loss of her child's father. With both of us beginning our program, we were reassured that our next calling would be greater than ourselves.

Operating in my last semester of school, mentoring, working, and understanding the fundamentals in beginning a business, I then heard once more the word MOVE! Again, hearing this word allowed me to become aggravated because I did not have a clue on where I would be moving to but I was obedient. Operating in obedience does not always provide you a clear picture to see where you are going but it is a matter of taking the first step to do so. Hearing the word "move" again felt as if I were given a second chance to do what I failed to do the first time. I felt that if I did not take advantage of the opportunity this time, then this could be my very last chance so I began to **MOVE**. Seeking positions in relation to counseling every day and submitting applications and resumes became a new job. I remember submitting 50 applications and only one employer called me wanting to conduct an interview. I was excited to know that the ball was in my court. All I had to do was interview well and I would get the job. Too easy, right?

Well come to find out my thought process was wrong. Although I interviewed well, I did not meet the specific state qualifications to work in that particular position. Instead, they offered me a receptionist position to get my foot in the door; however, they only wanted to pay me $8.00 an hour. Trying to wrap my mind around everything that was spoken to me, I did not know if this was a test of being humble or just a joke, but I was highly disappointed. My pay rate working at my present job was $11.35 an hour and in just 5 weeks I was going to graduate with my Masters with a 3.5 GPA. *Is this all that my life has to offer me?* I felt really offended because of all the schooling I had been through to get this far felt like a waste. The person then bargained with me and asked would I accept $9.00 an hour and as much as I wanted to say no, I said yes to hopefully get my foot into the door of joining the mental health field. The interviewer told me that she would have to ask her supervisor if she could pay $9.00 an hour and stated that she would be back in touch with me within a week. After the interview, I did not know how to feel.

Weeks passed by and I never heard back from the lady that interviewed me. Being desperate for an answer, I emailed her and called; however, I never got the chance to get in touch with her. So here it was back at square one not understanding how I would hear to move, but every move I took, the door would always shut. I went back to my daily routine of working full time, school, mentoring, and educating myself on business.

"My thoughts are nothing like your thoughts," says the Lord." (Isaiah 55:8 NLT)

- **My Lesson:** My thoughts are not always God's thoughts for my life.
- **My Blessing:** God blocked the opportunities that were not meant for me.
- **My Recipe:** When beginning to operate in my own will I need to stop and consult God.

~JOURNAL MY BLESSON~

Think of a time when you felt that every door that was open actually closed for you. How did you feel? What did you learn? How did your lesson serve as a blessing later in life? What recipe can you develop to help you move forward?

- ❖ Situation:

- ❖ Lesson:

- ❖ Blessing:

- ❖ Recipe:

Chapter 7

Blessons: Move Pt. 3

As graduation approached, I became more overwhelmed daily. I had a lot to juggle, taking four classes for eight weeks to graduate, working full time, typing 30-page papers in hours, mentoring, and catching up on sleep was a total disaster. On top of that, knowing that I would graduate yet with another degree to only work in a completely opposite field had me frustrated; frustrated to know that I did things the "All American Way." I finished high school and went straight to college and graduated in four years to expect to get a good paying job. Well, it did not work quite that way, so I decided to pursue a higher level of education and still found myself stuck in the same position.

There was a great part of me that knew I was going to resign from my current position at the credit union. It was not the fact that I did not like my job, but I believe that I felt as if there were no areas of growth for myself. My idea of moving up in positions for certain jobs required a person to be fired, die, or retire, and I did not want to see myself waiting for a moment as such. It was then I decided that it was time to move.

The day that I would resign from my current position was going to be on my 25th birthday because I then had vacation set up for a week and would only have to work one more week after. In the meantime, preparing for my transition prompted me to take advantage of every opportunity there was in the current positions that I held. With my transition this time, I was silent because I knew that the vision was in motion. I did not make a grand announcement to anyone other than three people I consulted with daily. I even held the information from my family members because I knew that although my family would have my best interest, they were going to be concerned with me leaving a job without having the plan of getting another therefore; I kept quiet.

It was the last week of school and I would graduate that Saturday on May 10th. As excited as I wanted to feel, I just could not due to being overwhelmed with writing 30-page papers and completing the last little bit of stuff before graduation, and on top of that I still had to work. Calling out was less of an option because I would have to visit a doctor and receive a note. This was not even worth my money or time, so I came into work frustrated and all. While speaking to my mentor, she noticed how horrible I appeared while discussing my process of transition with her. She asked me that particular day "Why wait until your birthday to leave if you plan on leaving anyway? Just put your notice in today she said." As much as this lady made sense it put so much pressure on me. I now had to make the biggest decision of my life: *Do I stay or move?*

Linking up with another person, we calculated my vacation time, and it only made sense to put my resignation letter in on that day and not take a vacation, because my vacation from the credit union would be no longer working there. I took a 30-minute lunch break outdoors and paced back forth, desperately seeking an answer. My heart was pounding and I clearly did not know what to do. I made one statement to God saying "If this is something that I am not supposed to do today, I need you to speak now!" For five minutes I paced up and down the sidewalk, hoping to hear something, but instead, I heard nothing.

I walked back into the building trembling and sat at my computer desk to change the date of my resignation letter stating May 16th would be my final day of work. I printed the letter off, signed it, and put it in the back to be delivered with the rest of the mail. I went to my mentor who was also next in command in my department and told her that I put in my resignation letter. She was shocked and she gave me a hug and asked me, "Are you sure you that this is what you want to do? Do you want to change your mind?" I then told her that it was my final decision. She then called the head boss to notify her that she would be receiving a resignation letter from me and that my last day would be May 16th. Word began to spread quickly and many people thought I was transitioning into another job as they always known me wanting to do, but little did they know that this time I was transitioning into the world of faith and entrepreneurship.

"For we live by believing and not by seeing"
(2 Corinthians 5:7 NLT)

- **My Lesson:** Trust your gut feeling.
- **My Blessing:** I was able to walk into the next journey to life.
- **My Recipe:** To remember that I have the wisdom and knowledge to make decisions and will also walk by faith and not by sight.

~JOURNAL MY BLESSON~

Think of a time when you decided to take a leap of faith, what happened? What did you learn? How did your lesson serve as a blessing later in life? What recipe can you develop to help you move forward?

- ❖ Situation:

- ❖ Lesson:

- ❖ Blessing:

- ❖ Recipe:

Chapter 8

Blessons: Entrepreneur Like and Follow

In the world today, everyone has a social media page whether it is Facebook, Instagram, Twitter, or LinkedIn. We tend to use some type of media platform to promote ourselves and business. It is very often when we create these pages, we utilize hash tags and taglines that say like my page and follow us. The reality behind social media is that you will have some people who actually like and follow you because they truly support you, and then you will have others that like and follow you to just be nosey.

When I began my first business, I expected everyone to like and follow my page and to also donate to my nonprofit because we were dedicated to making a change with the youth within our community. I was desperate to gain the support of people and wanted everyone to follow the move and help; however, there were people that followed to unfollow my page and my business post were only liked by the same few supporting friends. Talk about aggravated! Why would someone unfollow my page and not even support our youth in the community? I mean, I was doing a good deed, right?

After one year of building and running my business page finally reaching over 900 likes, I became content not knowing the test that I would have to face in the following year. My business page was connected to my regular profile in which was hacked. Not only losing my personal profile page filled with high school and college memories, but I also lost my entire business page that contained 900 likes! Once again, I became aggravated. Does anyone have anything better to do than to hack pages on social media? Looking at this situation today allows me to have the understanding that you sometimes have to lose to win again and likes are not even a serious matter. People know who I am, the name of the business, and what I have accomplished, whether they have liked the page or not.

Losing my business page served as a real humbling moment for me, it allowed me to open my eyes and ask myself: Did I go into business to please people or to be of service? Entrusted with the plan of aspiring both at risk and willing youth, allows me to realize that it is my duty to do that whether I have the support of individuals or not. Going through this provided me understanding that when operating in a plan that is not your own, you will be provided with all the tools necessary to succeed.

"And this same God who takes care of me will supply all your needs from his glorious riches, which have been given to us in Christ Jesus." (Philippians 4:29 NLT)

- **My Lesson:** Never put your hope into likes, social media, or people because it will leave you disappointed.
- **My Blessing:** I was able to develop growth within myself.
- **My Recipe:** Keep your eye on the prize and focus on what matters the most.

~JOURNAL MY BLESSON~

Think of a time when you had so much hope in a person that let you down. What happened? What did you learn? How did your lesson serve as a blessing later in life? What recipe can you develop to help you move forward?

- ❖ Situation:

- ❖ Lesson:

- ❖ Blessing:

- ❖ Recipe:

Chapter 9

Blessons: Caught in the Hype of Entrepreneurship

Entrepreneurship seems to be the new wave that everyone has jumped on in the past few years, including myself. Some people were built for corporate jobs where others were built to run their own businesses. Whether you work in corporate America or an entrepreneur; either is fine, as long as **YOU ARE SATISFIED**.

It is so easy to get caught up with the ways of the world and social media. Social media can be utilized to make becoming an entrepreneur glamorous, stress, and worry free, and to just live your best life! While all of this can be true, the real fact of the matter is: nobody ever displays the struggle. The struggle of trying to generate startup funding for your business, sustaining your business, hiring great employees, targeting your population, processing legal documents, attracting paying clients, and so much more. **DO NOT BELIEVE ALL OF THE HYPE BECAUSE THE STRUGGLE IS REAL!**

There is also a displayed mindset where you have to go and "secure the bag or make them coins," work 24/7 to become successful, no sleep, brand daily, secure seven streams of income, exercise, drink water, and work hard to play harder. As I do believe in some of these sayings, I also believe in taking time out for **YOU**. How effective can you be running a business or working when you choose to operate 24/7? How can you secure the bag with seven streams of income fatigue? Would you really be giving your best image of your brand under these conditions? Although it may seem possible, I believe that there will be some lack somewhere in life.

Stepping out into the scene of entrepreneurship with my first business as a nonprofit, I was super excited. Following seven-figured entrepreneurs on social media and trying to mimic their entrepreneurial ways, gave me hope that I to would have seven-figures. My business endeavors excited me so much that it kept me up working until 4:00 a.m. to only be back up in the next three hours doing it all over. Even when I was so-called resting, I really was not because my mind was steadily racing about the next big idea for the business. This may sound like I was really dedicated to my business in which I was; however, I did not know when and how to shut it off and I became married to entrepreneurship.

During this time, I developed new habits that didn't allow me to enjoy myself unless it was business related, only feeling comfortable of meeting people on a business level rather than personal, spending less time with loved ones, and constantly investing myself in many workshops and classes offered for business. In the mist of my ambition, there were major sacrifices. I will never say that all of these things that I experienced did not help me become more of an effective person today; I just wished that I could have enjoyed the true journey in the beginning stages of freedom.

From the age of 16, I had my very first job and from then on, I was always employed with at least two or even three jobs. It is not that I had to work all of these jobs, I just chose to live a certain type of lifestyle. I knew the value of work without the shadow of a doubt, but what I did not know was how to apply the value of time and self-care. I learned the hard way that time is of the essence. We can take time to build our empire daily, but it is also essential for us to sit down, reflect and enjoy the presence of others, celebrate accomplishments, complete a self-inventory, become one with nature, become whole with God, spend time with your loved ones, enjoy a home-cooked meal, and of all, log off social media from time to time.

It is so easy to get caught up with living in the fast lane of being busy and focusing on what others are doing where it then becomes a nonstop working comparison struggle, one that we will never win. I learned that it was imperative to create my own recipe for success through the lens of **MY PROCESS**! I wholeheartedly believe that each of us was brought into this world with a special purpose and that each individual should be responsible of never losing sight of that. The main ingredients developed in our process will help develop the recipes to our own success.

Throughout my process, I understand that it takes much dedication and hard work to become successful in life, but it is also wise to understand to take pleasure in the little things and enjoy. For me, taking a mental health day is well needed because as much as the enemy likes an idle mind, he loves a busy one too.

"Don't copy the behavior and customs of this world, but let God transform you into a new person by changing the way you think. Then you will learn to know God's will for you, which is good and pleasing and perfect."
(Romans 12:2 NLT)

- **My Lesson:** I learned that it does not always work with following someone else's path to success and to stop putting so much focus and emphasis on it.
- **My Blessing:** I am able to pull away from work when it seems that it is overwhelming.
- **My Recipe:** When I become so consumed in work, I need to recognize and take a step back and recharge.

~JOURNAL MY BLESSON~

Think of a time in life that you were caught up in the hype of doing something because of what you saw displayed. What happened? What did you learn? How did your lesson serve as a blessing later in life? What recipe can you develop to help you move forward?

- ❖ Situation:

- ❖ Lesson:

- ❖ Blessing:

- ❖ Recipe:

Chapter 10

Blessons: Entrepreneur Set Your Price and Be Quiet

As an entrepreneur, how many times has a person asked how much your product or service was? Many of you would probably say quite frequently. Now my next question is: How many times have you told them your actual price, but then offered a lower price? Again, some of you may answer yes, as I am guilty of doing it myself. Why do we do this? Well, I now realize the reason as to why because this person was once me.

You probably would agree that there are some rough times in business. Sales may be up one month and take a huge plummet in the next month. Business based on the economy can just be unpredictable, so every time I received a client referral and they asked my price; I would often discount it. In desperate need of sales, I felt that if my prices were lowered, I could secure funding and bring more clientele to my company. Although this seemed to have worked for a little while, I then began to notice how much money I was losing out on and often felt like I was selling myself short. There was nobody to blame but myself.

Whether in business or life, you cannot allow anything to control you; whether that being money, people, or materialistic things. Clients that really desire your service will respect your prices. With this understanding, I have learned to present myself well, state my price, and be quiet.

Doing this gives the client the opportunity to decide if they want to conduct business with you or not. In any business that you pursue, you cannot always fully satisfy everyone and their needs; however, you can provide excellent service. People may not remember what you have said, but they will always remember how you made them feel. This has been the ultimate key for me in creating long-lasting relationships with my clients and the primary reason why they return.

"So don't be afraid; you are more valuable to God than a whole flock of sparrows." (Matthew 10:31 NLT)

- **My Lesson:** Know your worth, set your price, and be quiet.
- **My Blessing:** I was able to become confident in charging my worth.
- **My Recipe:** When I feel the need to discount my service, I need to seek within and ask myself why am I doing it.

~JOURNAL MY BLESSON~

Think of a time when you offered a discount. Did you feel as if you were obligated to do so? What did you learn? How did your lesson serve as a blessing later in life? What recipe can you develop to help you move forward?

- ❖ Situation:

- ❖ Lesson:

- ❖ Blessing:

- ❖ Recipe:

Chapter: 11

Blessons: Qualified by Purpose

Take a look at today, what are the things the world says that we need to have in order to be qualified? Some things that may come to mind may be the completion of high school, a college degree, certification, or even a license. While all of these things enhance our portfolios and resumes, do you think they actually qualify us as experts?

The years of pursuing a higher level of education is something that I personally value. To obtain a costly piece of paper and many letters of the alphabet behind my name took many nights of blood, sweat, tears, sacrifice, and obedience. I can admit, it was a great rewarding experience that many may or may not be interested in, but what if I told you that the same piece of paper that qualifies me would amount to the same things that you already have been prequalified for by purpose?

Growing up, I found myself like a few others living the "All American Standard." Do well in high school, go to college, and finish on time, and you will be destined for success and greatness in a career. Well let's just say that standard was cut short once I realized I was qualified for my career field because of a piece of paper, but in actuality I was underqualified when it came to experience.

We live in a world where a degree does hold the value that you may be educated in the line of work for your career field, but it does not necessarily mean that you are "qualified to perform." For instance, who do you think would land the job of a Crime Scene Technician, the college graduate that obtained their Bachelor's Degree in Forensic Science with nearly any hands-on experience, or the retired deputy sheriff with no degree and 10+ years of experience? More than likely, you may find the person with 10+ years of experience to land the job. The reason why I say this is because this college graduate applying for this job was once me. Although I believe that I could have been as effective as someone of 10+ years in the line of duty I was only chosen for an interview because of the completion of my degree. Do we need a degree or experience?

Take the time to think about the people you know that have held high positions and technically were not qualified, but for whatever reason they got the position? A scenario like this would be referred to as purpose in which each of us have. Your purpose could be to one day become President or become the world's most renowned philanthropist who knows. You have to be accepting that your ultimate calling makes you qualified and many people will disagree.

Do we really need to be qualified for the positions stated above? Although having a degree and experiences prepare you for certain careers, your ultimate purpose and gifts within you can also carry the same value.

Pursuing passion and purpose will make you more of a valuable asset, and also enhances your abilities to become the best you. Your purpose is what makes you, while your experiences are what mold and shapes you, and education adds another version to you.

"But God chose the foolish things of the world to shame the wise; God chose the weak things of the world to shame the

strong. God chose the lowly things of this world and the despised things—and the things that are not—to nullify the things that are, so that no one may boast before him."
(1 Corinthians 1:27-29 NLT)

- **My Lesson:** An expert is not always the one that has a degree or certification; they could be a person pursuing purpose.
- **My Blessing:** I have the understanding that I have been prequalified in certain areas in life that I do not have any expertise in, and that I need to exercise those gifts.
- **My Recipe:** Use the gifts that I already have to produce growth.

~JOURNAL MY BLESSON~

Think of a time when you received something knowingly that you were unqualified. How did you feel? What did you learn? How did your lesson serve as a blessing later in life? What recipe can you develop to help you move forward?

- ❖ Situation:

- ❖ Lesson:

- ❖ Blessing:

- ❖ Recipe:

Chapter 12

Blessons: Experience is the Best Key

Would you believe that each and every one of your experiences have molded you to become the person that you are today? Your thought process, response, attitude, mindset, expectations, and behavior are all shaped by your experiences. Through the process of life, you will discover how your experiences have helped you with certain areas and how they have affected you in other areas, but what matters overall is how you work through the process.

As I look back upon all of my experiences, I realize that they have taught me empathy, sympathy, patience, understanding, leadership, integrity, as well as social and interpersonal skills. Many of these learned experiences came from the different positions that I held when working a job. My first job at the age of 16 was at a fast food restaurant. Working fast food taught me great customer service, cash handling, proper communication, promptness, and professionalism. After working fast food for a couple of months, I then transitioned to working retail.

Working retail was not only my dream job at the age of 16, but it was a job where I applied each of my skillsets from the previous job and added more which then made me more effective and valuable in retail and commission sales. In the retail industry, I learned how to become an effective leader, upsell products, knowledgeable in inventory, stocking and restocking, merchandising, product knowledge, credit approval, teamwork, arranging displays, advising, product demonstration, management and pricing.

The final job that I worked before becoming an entrepreneur was at the credit union. In addition to the skills listed above, I was able to gain experience in selling banking products and services, answering inbound calls, training new employees, maintain federal banking guidelines, complete management paperwork in a timely manner, cash accountability, and responsibility.

Evaluating my entrepreneurial role today, allows me to understand that my experiences were exactly what I needed to effectively run a business. From great customer service to selling products, budgeting, and cash management were just some of the most important things needed to become an entrepreneur. While working a corporate job I knew that I had to maximize what was in my hands at the present moment even if that meant attending leadership meetings or accepting additional training without an incentive; this was all a part of the process.

'And we know that God causes everything to work together[a] for the good of those who love God and are called according to his purpose for them."
(Romans 8:28 NLT)

- **My Lesson:** Seek the benefit in every circumstance.
- **My Blessing:** I was able to learn and develop many skillsets while working a job.
- **My Recipe:** Utilize every opportunity to advance you to the next level.

~JOURNAL MY BLESSON~

How has your experiences molded you into the person that you are today? What did you learn in the process? How did your lesson serve as a blessing later in life? What recipe can you develop to help you move forward?

- ❖ Situation:

- ❖ Lesson:

- ❖ Blessing:

- ❖ Recipe:

Chapter: 13

Blessons: Beauty in Brokenness

It is very often when we hear the word abuse that we correlate it to something that is physically related rather than taking in consideration of the mental and emotional aspects. Physical, mental, and emotional abuse often travel together. Physical abuse is harmful but mental and emotional abuse can be just as worse.

Take a second to think if you have ever been mentally or emotionally abused by anyone? Did you bother to seek help? Roughly a good number of people do not report mental or emotional abuse because they tend to blame themselves for being abused. There are times in life where we build our own perception of ourselves based on the way that others view us. Once a mental abuser is able to realize that they have this control, it then provides them with the opportunity to manipulate the individual into thinking that they are inadequate or always to blame.

The power that someone has over you can be unrecognizable until you notice that your heart begins to race when you see them passing by, the thought of them alters your behavior, or you happen to see one of their family members and you realize the hate that you carry within. Your next question may be how could a person make you feel as such? My answer would be because I allowed them to.

The beginning of a failed relationship felt so fulfilling and exciting where I missed a lot of the warning signs in the process. I avoided stating the obvious because I did not want to seem as if I was nagging, ignored the signs of truth, gave the person multiple chances when they only deserved one, and of all began to think that there was something wrong with me and blamed myself. The only thing that was wrong with me in this picture is the amount of time I allowed this behavior to continue. I was emotionally consumed with the relationship where my life was completely out of order. I put the person that said they loved me before God, his family before mine, and myself last.

It was not until a few months of going through the same cycle I realized that I became very depressed, angry, and isolated from the world all while trying to appear normal working a full-time job and attending school. My emotional abuse was often masked with work and a smile but deep down inside I felt as if I was diminishing away silently.

As much as I was trying to fight the battle within my own will, I often felt defeated, until one night I was in my room and was mentally tired. Before you know it, I fell to my knees for the first time during the process pleading for help. That particular moment allowed me to realize that it was not only an emotional and mental battle that I was encountering, but the heaviness of the issue became spiritual. God was waiting on me to cast my cares upon Him so that He could begin my healing process. After seven months of fighting a fight that God did not assign, I found myself with a new alignment.... God, Self, Family, and then everything else.

And the one sitting on the throne said, "Look, I am making everything new!" And then he said to me, "Write this down, for what I tell you is trustworthy and true."
(Revelation 21:5 NLT)

- **My Lesson:** I now recognize that there are some things that we bring upon ourselves due to being caught in the feeling or the moment.
- **My Blessing:** I was able to experience a major breakthrough and find myself again.
- **My Recipe:** When I become so consumed in my problems, I need to recognize that I have put my issues before God and I need to consult him.

~JOURNAL MY BLESSON~

Think of a time in life that you were mentally, physically, or emotionally abused. How did you overcome? What did you learn? How did your lesson serve as a blessing later in life? What recipe can you develop to help you move forward?

- ❖ Situation:

- ❖ Lesson:

- ❖ Blessing:

- ❖ Recipe

Chapter 14

Blessons: The Masked Runner

In my past time, I enjoy running miles because it helps me improve both my physical and mental well-being. I loved running so much that I soon became a masked professional runner. My definition of a masked professional runner is not a person that participates in marathons, but a person that does not want to deal with particular things in life; therefore, they mask it behind something that seems normal to the average person. The professional runner being described was me. I ran from people, hurt, family, truth, and masked it all with work. Work was not only a mask for me but it served as my safety net. Work was more than a 9-5, it was school, business ideas, accomplishing goals, and constantly preparing for the near future.

The first time my busyness became unmasked was in the time period that my grandmother was passing. It was May of 2015, where my sisters and I visit my grandmother for Mother's Day and noticed a change, but we did not become that concerned. Weeks later, she was placed in the hospital for one thing which then escalated to other things. The next time that I would see and hear from my grandmother would be next to her hospital bed. During this time, I was pursuing a business as well as attending graduate school.

With everything going on with my grandmother in the hospital, I made it a priority to drive an hour in a half each day to see her. One particular day, I brought my laptop to the hospital hoping to complete my schoolwork, but instead, I was using it to try and take my mind off of my grandmother's condition. Knowingly in my heart I knew that it was her time any day, as her health seemed to decline, but I did not want to register that in my mind; therefore, I tried to work through the truth, my family, and my pain.

After about a week of visiting my grandmother she was then released from the hospital and placed in home hospice. As much as I wanted to drive to go see her at home, I knew that I needed to complete my final and a paper. As a family, we had planned to go down and visit together on that Saturday which would have been the Fourth of July; but instead, plans were changed and everyone went to visit on that Friday without me. I was upset, but I knew that my semester was ending, so it was imperative that I finished out the semester strong and complete my assignments. Rescheduling my grandmothers visit to Sunday allowed me to meet my deadlines for school, but little did I know that it would be the day I received a phone call stating that she took her last breath that morning. I was devastated, angry, and of all, sad because my grandmother was gone and I felt like I did not have the opportunity to say goodbye.

A few days went by, and then before you know it, it was the day of the funeral. On this day I remember my spiritual sister calling me to give her condolences and to pray for me. I thanked her and told her that I was going to pack my laptop so I could get some work done, and then she said, "Christen!" I answered, "What?" She said, "This is a time period that you need to be with your family." She continued and shared that I needed to take some time for myself and grieve. Tears begin to flow from my eyes as I knew this was true, but it was then I realized I had been masking the pain, hurt, and sorrow of my grandmother's passing all behind a mask called work.

Rest in peace, Golden Girl.

'He will wipe every tear from their eyes. There will be no more death' or mourning or crying or pain, for the old order of things has passed away." (Revelation 21:4 NLT)

- **My Lesson:** Dealing with situations in life grows our character and strength.
- **My Blessing:** Learning that masking situations does not help with healing and how seeking a grief support group helps.
- **My Recipe:** When I feel like putting on a mask, conduct a self-check and ask why.

~JOURNAL MY BLESSON~

Think of a time when you put on a mask for something that you did not want to deal with? What did you learn? How did your lesson serve as a blessing later in life? What recipe can you develop to help you move forward?

- ❖ Situation:

- ❖ Lesson:

- ❖ Blessing:

- ❖ Recipe:

Chapter 15

Blessons: Pass or Fail

How many tests in life do you ever recall failing? One, two, three, four, or maybe even more. Believe it or not, we all have tests weekly and even daily. Some tests are conducted by paper and pencil, where other tests may be conducted by computer, but what about those special tests? You know, the tests that build your character to make you stronger, or how about the tests that says you failed but you actually passed?

It was a gloomy day leaving my house to travel and sit for what I thought was the most important test in my life, which was the National Counseling Exam (NCE). After 4 ½ years of graduate school, certifications, experience, and well prepared, I figured it was time to begin my journey as a Licensed Professional Counselor. Passing this test to me meant becoming a Licensed Professional Counselor Associate (LPCA) that could begin earning accumulated hours to become fully licensed, beginning my own private practice, financial stability, and of all, finally working in my career field after 8 ½ years of post-secondary education. This test meant the most, and I did everything in my power to properly prepare for it.

I remember constantly speaking affirmations that day because my anxiety level was high. I checked into the city an hour before my exam, but with troubles of finding my test site as my GPS kept directing me to a neighborhood. It was

6:00 a.m. and I rode around the neighborhood about ten times to find the location, praying that I would see someone to verify directions. I began to panic and finally, 30 minutes later I saw a woman walking her dog, so I decided to ask her for directions. She explained to me that I was in the right place; however, in the wrong area. She told me that the GPS and maps online had not been updated which often confused many people. Once receiving the new directions, I quickly drove over with only 15 minutes to check in. I finally checked in and my anxiety was not only high because I thought that I would miss my exam, but I felt like I went through the roof when I discovered that this was an electronic exam. Prepared for a pencil and paper format exam to only see a room filled with 12 computers was a shock for me. The security process was enough in itself as well.

It took me exactly 4 hours to complete the exam, and even in those four hours I felt as if I did not have enough time, but I finished, and that was all that mattered to me. I figured I could just forget about the whole process and enjoy my day as I thought the scores would be mailed weeks later....I was wrong. The scores were printed instantly. With my heart racing, my name was called and the testing coordinator handed me my results. I flipped over the paper to only see my name and beside it was the word, FAILED.

My body went into an instant shock because I knew that I took the time to study everything that I needed to successfully pass this exam, but the piece of paper I held in my hand said otherwise. Leaving the testing site walking down the hallway with no expression or thought, I stepped outside the double doors and it began to rain. Still emotionless, I got into my car and took a deep breath and said, "Lord I still trust You." it was right then and there the tears began to fall from my eyes.

Moving forward from this day, I realized that it was not about me passing a test for my license, it was about me passing the test of trusting God even when He does not give you what you want or when you want it. Although my paper said FAILED, God said I PASSED!

"Trust in the Lord with all your heart; do not depend on your own understanding." (Proverbs 3:5 NLT)

- **My Lesson:** Your timing is not always God's timing.
- **My Blessing:** Learning how to overcome failure.
- **My Recipe:** Seek clarity in the plans that God has for you when you begin making your own plans for your life.

~JOURNAL MY BLESSON~

Think of a time when you wanted something so bad and you did not get it because it was not the right time? What did you learn? How did your lesson serve as a blessing later in life? What recipe can you develop to help you move forward?

- ❖ Situation:

- ❖ Lesson:

- ❖ Blessing:

- ❖ Recipe:

Chapter 16

Blessons: The Power in Healing

In some part of our lives we will find that we will go through the process of grief. Grief is a natural reaction to death and is identified in five common stages: denial, anger, bargaining, depression, and acceptance. During the process of grief, many of us may find that we are still broken within because we have not properly healed and gone through each stage of grief.

Denial is the first stage of grief and is often the first reaction in learning about the death or illness of a loved one or someone known. During this stage, it is hard to accept the nature of reality; therefore; it is common to block out anything that does not make sense and become numb towards what does. Anger is associated with the second stage of grief. Once denial begins to disappear is when anger sets in. You may find yourself angry and direct it towards everyone.

Bargaining is the third stage of grief. In this stage you begin to ask yourself what you could or should have done to prevent the loss. After bargaining, the depression stage sets in. At this time, you begin to understand how the loss affects your life. The feelings associated with depression are isolation, crying, sleep deprivation, decreased appetite, loneliness, and feelings of being overwhelmed. The final stage of grief is acceptance, and it is at this stage where you learn to accept the reality of the loss. You accept the things that you cannot change and work on things that you can to promote self-healing.

It was not until a week before my 30th birthday where I would finally reach the stage of acceptance and find peace with the death of my college friend murdered the day after my birthday. In my own process of grief, I often felt angry, questioned why, and blamed myself for not attending the funeral, and even faced some periods of depression, especially each year when my birthday came. I not only had to deal with my emotions for six years, but I had to be very respectful of my spiritual sister's emotions because this dear friend of mine that was no longer here was my spiritual sister's first love and child's father. Could you even imagine how hard it was for her to celebrate my birthday and knowing that the next day she would have to look into her daughters' eyes and catch every tear all while comforting her?

Each year I wanted to go visit the burial site, but for whatever reason I never made it down there. I vowed a promise to my dear friend and self that in the year we celebrated our 30th birthday is when I would conquer what I had been running from which was acceptance and closure. A week before my birthday, I took a 2-hour ride to the burial site of my dear friend. Upon approaching the scene, I automatically converted back to the denial stage of grief.

Sitting in the grass for 30 minutes, allowed me to begin to process the reality of what I had been running from. My dear friend's name was on a card that read the date of sunrise, and date of sunset and that is when I suddenly cried. I began to talk to my dear friend as if he stood in front of me for two hours using a form of therapy to assist with my healing process. Conquering this hurt and fear allowed me to realize that the six-year buildup of tears and sorrow had now been restored with acceptance, peace, and overall wholeness.

"He heals the brokenhearted and bandages their wounds." (Psalm 147:3 NLT)

- **My Lesson**: There is a process when it comes to healing.
- **My Blessing**: I was able to let go of pain and be restored with peace.
- **My Recipe:** When the process seems heavy, still find that sense of hope and trust God that He will help us in our time of need.

~JOURNAL MY BLESSON~

Think of a time when you experienced grief. What was your experience? What did you learn? How did your lesson serve as a blessing later in life? What recipe can you develop to help you move forward?

- ❖ Situation:

- ❖ Lesson:

- ❖ Blessing:

- ❖ Recipe:

Chapter 17

Blessons: The Day I Married Myself

Last summer, I challenged myself to run my first 100k in which I had the entire summer to do. My main focus for the summer was body goals for fall, and was very adamant about reaching them. As I began my timer and focused on running up the hill, I heard the words: marry yourself. At first, I was a little puzzled, but then I digested exactly what was being spoken to me.

Earlier in that week, I viewed wedding dresses online. There were so many beautiful dresses but there were only two that I fell in love with. One of the dresses exposed all of my back and as much as I liked it, I knew that I would not be confident in wearing it, because over the years, my back was not as flat and smooth as it once was. I asked myself: *Who wants to see a person in a wedding dress with a back roll?* I used this thought as a sense of motivation for me to complete my 100k. Although a negative thought was turned into a positive action, I was shown something a little deeper than surface level.

The *Bridezilla* show is a prime example of how stressful things could be for a woman preparing for her wedding day. Even though we may have a wedding planner, there are still some of us that like to be in the mix of our wedding plans to make sure everything is perfect. The question is: Do we want things perfect for ourselves or perfect for our audience? Think about it, the dress gave me motivation to work out but my entire thought process, was about how others would perceive me if my back was not flat wearing the dress that I liked. It is so easy to prepare for something and make it grand for the liking of others, but what about ourselves? There are many of us that find ourselves constantly working out, starving, going on diets to only first meet the expectation of how others see us. While some of this may be true there is also a part of us that negatively impacts ourselves just with our own self talk and thoughts.

The thoughtful moment of being told to marry myself, allowed me to gain a deeper understanding of self-love. If I desired to look a certain way for my next event, then that is up to me, but learning to never allow the opinions of others to affect how I view myself was the ultimate lesson. I took a vow in the mirror that day and said, "I do."

"To acquire wisdom is to love yourself; people who cherish understand will prosper." (Proverbs 19:8 NLT)

- **My Lesson**: Be confident in who you are.
- **My Blessing**: Focusing more on self-love.
- **My Recipe:** When it seems like you are getting into a place to satisfy others check your motives.

~JOURNAL MY BLESSON~

Think of a time when you realized that you needed to put yourself first. How was your experience? What did you learn? How did your lesson serve as a blessing later in life? What recipe can you develop to help you move forward?

- ❖ Situation:

- ❖ Lesson:

- ❖ Blessing:

- ❖ Recipe:

Chapter 18

Blessons: Out with the Old

Have you ever held onto something that was so worn down, and you carried the mindset that since it was not broke, it did not need to be fixed or replaced? I know I have; from a pair of comfy heels to ripped jeans, I just wanted to keep wearing them because there was a sense of comfort, but there would be one day that I would have to step outside of my comfort zone.

It is very often that we pray for new things with the intentions of keeping the old things, and sometimes that method does not work. I prayed to get a new vehicle, but I wanted to do so in my timing. You see my timing consisted of having enough money to afford a new vehicle, because going back to a 9-5 was not an option for me. My timing also consisted of eliminating as much debt as I could and to save. Although this may have worked temporarily, it was not the answer to my problem once my engine died on the highway in my car.

I remember buying my car brand new straight off the lot in 2008. This was my second vehicle, but the first one that I was responsible for making payments for. I took great care of my car and had very minor issues along the years. In the last 10 years, I had to do very little maintenance with this vehicle because I took care of it and it took care of me.

One day, I happened to be traveling on I-95 where a raccoon laid in the road as if it were dead. I figured instead of jumping in the lane beside me with other vehicles, I would just roll over it instead of running over it. Approaching the raccoon, I thought was dead, it stood up! I screamed, and the next thing I heard was thump, thump, thump; I then knew that the raccoon was now deceased. I prayed that there was no damage to my vehicle, but after getting home, I discovered damage to the front bumper. I was livid because a car that was paid off for five years and rarely needed maintenance; now needed a new bumper.

I asked myself: *What did I look like as a business owner riding around with a messed-up bumper?* I did some shopping around, and of course everything was out of my budget around Christmas time, so I decided to wait after the holidays and get it fixed. Still riding around with the same bumper in February of 2018, I then experienced something else with my vehicle. As I rode down the highway on another occasion, I noticed that my car would not accelerate, so I then pulled over in enough time before the entire vehicle shut down and found myself alongside of the road for hours. Eventually proper aid arrived and I did not have to wait by myself. First the bumper, and now this! After hours of waiting my vehicle was towed, and I was then on my way home, to think about how expensive this process was going to be. At this point, I no longer cared about the bumper; I just wanted my old car up and running.

A few days at the shop, I received a phone call stating some news I did not want to hear. I was told that my entire engine would need to be replaced, my heart dropped. Who was prepared to pay for an engine or much less think about getting a new vehicle with payments? I was so overwhelmed that I just got the vehicle towed back home. I had to make decisions, and although it felt like the wrong timing, this was my chance to get the new vehicle that I wanted, or I also had the option of purchasing a brand-new engine for about 3k and pray that nothing else happened to my car. I had no idea what to do, but the number one blessing about it was that I had a vehicle to drive in my process of finding another one to call my own.

I tried not to think about the situation, as many would ask what were my plans were. I simply did not know; therefore, I gave no answer. One wise person then told me I should take some time and think about what I wanted to do and to not rush the process, because it was not like I did not have a vehicle to drive to and from. This was true, so I barely brought up the subject of what I would do next. During the month of March was when I decided I was going to get a new vehicle. I could not see myself purchasing a brand new or old engine, and then something else would go wrong. So now my heart was set upon a new vehicle, what to get, where to get it, the price range, and how I was going to afford it, and of course when to get it. Weeks of shopping around allowed me to narrow my search down to three vehicles. From the three vehicles, I was then able to narrow it down to one, and determined that I wanted to get my vehicle on my 30th birthday.

Now that I had a plan in place, I did not worry, because I knew that it was going to happen and that I had a 6-day trip to prepare for. I went to the Bahamas with a bunch of friends and family, and we had an enjoyable time. Reality only hit me when I came back and realized that I still did not have a vehicle of my own. My spiritual sister then told me to stop putting a date on my blessings. She said you do not have to wait until your birthday to get a new vehicle, you can get one today! Even though I was not going to get a vehicle on that particular day, I did understand what she was saying.

The next two weeks, I shopped around, looking for the best deals for the vehicle that I wanted. The price, mileage, and the color of the vehicle mattered to me, and I was not going to settle for anything less. I found a vehicle out of town, and reserved to look at it for that next day, but the dealership ended up calling me to tell me that somebody had bought it and asked if I would be interested in another color and I declined. At this point, I was over the process of looking, until the next week the same particular vehicle in my price range, located closer to me, and a beautiful color appeared in my search. The dealership soon contacted me, and before you know, I was test driving the vehicle and fell in love with it.

We then began the paperwork process, and the manager of the dealership asked me some questions before he pulled my credit. I gave him a ballpark of where I wanted my payments and an estimated value of my credit score that I was not for sure of. Sitting in the office as calm as could be, knowing that if I could not get the vehicle right then, there was a reason, and I was okay with it. The manager then ran my credit score and surprised me with news that it was 70 points higher than the estimated value I provided, but then he also gave me news that although my credit was good, he could not provide me a loan because the amount of loans I carried from school.

Once this statement was made, I thanked him for his time and was heading out the door until he asked me if I wanted to give my bank a shot. I sat down and said why not, and gave them a call and it was in three minutes that I was approved for a vehicle loan through my bank with a great APR and on top of that there was no down payment required, I knew then that my prayers were answered. When man said no, God worked everything out for my good. During this process, I learned that new things do not come the way we intend for them to come. We all have the opportunity to be qualified for anything new in life but some of us rarely get there because of the level of our comfort. Operating in comfort only forfeits the opportunity of experiencing new blessings.

- **My Lesson**: In order for new blessings to come, there has to be a willingness to give up what is old to make room for the new.
- **My Blessing**: I was able to walk out of a dealership with a new vehicle, great APR with no down payment.
- **My Recipe:** When I realize that I am holding to something so tight and cannot seem to let it go, I need to ask myself: *Have I gotten too comfortable?*

~JOURNAL MY BLESSON~

Think of a time when you had to give up something that you felt comfortable with, what was this experience like? What did you learn? How did your lesson serve as a blessing later in life? What recipe can you develop to help you move forward?

- ❖ Situation:

- ❖ Lesson:

- ❖ Blessing:

- ❖ Recipe:

Chapter 19

Blessons: Spiritual Food

It was Black Friday when I decided to go out of town to shop for Christmas gifts. Although I did not really want to deal with the traffic, people, and the test of my patience waiting, to be checked out in a long line, I am glad I went. I not only caught major sales, spent some time with myself, but I had a spiritual encounter through the spark of conversation and dinner.

On Black Friday, I only shopped in two stores because that was all that I could take. Before heading back home, I decided to dine in at one of my favorite restaurants and ordered my favorite dish which was the bourbon honey glazed salmon and mashed potatoes, in addition to the salad bar. Patiently waiting, I decided to call my spiritual sister. We shared some experiences and some stories that made us laugh, but one thing we both agreed upon was that we were both being called to a higher level.

The month of November, I took a break from consulting one-on-one sessions with my clients as I needed a break. It was my time to revisit, revamp, and reevaluate all the areas in my life. Once I was able to get into a quiet space, I was then revealed that my life was changing for the good. Although I enjoyed working one-on-one consulting and it became lucrative, I was shown something deeper. My purpose was more than consulting and coaching individuals to build their nonprofits; I was being led to help people in developing their mindset in the process. Just think for a second, how can you do anything in life without first having the right mindset? The business that I solely focused on, coaching and nonprofit consulting had now been altered to focusing on ministry/counseling with the addition to business coaching and consulting.

I explained this to my spiritual sister, and she too was feeling the same exact way when it came to ministry. We both saw ourselves not as ministers in the pulpit, but more of ministers outside of the four walls. It was a part of us where we had to admit to one another of how we really felt upon this ministry calling. Personally, I felt I have not fully answered this calling, because there were certain pieces of me that I wanted to hang on to. I enjoy consuming wine here and there, having a fun time with my girls, and even enjoy listening to certain music from time to time. Although these acts do not make me a horrible person, I often asked myself: *Would I still be considered a minister because I was not perfect?*

In the midst of the conversation, my phone died and the other part of my dinner came out. It looked delicious! I quickly dove in the mashed potatoes which were great, and cut a piece of my salmon realizing that it was not only warm, but it was not thoroughly cooked. I then notified my waitress, and she apologized to me and had a new meal prepared. Normally I would request to speak to a manager due to the inconvenience, but this particular day I did not do anything but wait patiently. The manager came to me and apologized reassuring me that I had another meal being prepared and it would be done correctly. My meal then came out in a to go box and before I left, I looked at my food to make sure that I was well satisfied. As I tried to grab the attention of my waitress for my check, she then told me that everything was taken care of. I thanked her, gave her a tip, and was soon back on the road.

Traveling back in silence, it was then I heard God speak to me once more just by the situation that just occurred with my salmon. Although we may not be perfected in our calling, God will still continue to use and prune us along the way. It was as if I was the glazed salmon that appeared to look good on the outside but on the inside, I was not fully cooked because I was developing in the process and during each time God took me back to make me well done. Instead of being referenced as a piece of salmon this process can be better recognized as GRACE that we are given. Grace does not give us the excuse to do what we want to do; however, it is through divine favor we are forgiven and given another chance to do the things we have been called to do. It is so easy to get put on a pedestal of perfection by ourselves and others, and in all, it hinders us in becoming the person that we have been called to become. You never know how you will be used to help others in the midst of your addiction, diagnosis, or circumstances, but I learned to never underestimate the power and impact of your calling because of your own thoughts of perfectionism.

"Not a single person on earth is always good and never sins" (Ecclesiastes 7:20 NLT)

- **Lesson**: No matter how hard we try in life we must realize that nobody is perfect.
- **Blessing**: I am now able to move forth within my calling of ministry.
- **Recipe**: When feeling unqualified to do certain things in life, seek the word instead of the world.

~JOURNAL MY BLESSON~

Think of a time in your life when you were called to do something but you held yourself back due to not feeling qualified. What did you learn? How did your lesson serve as a blessing later in life? What recipe can you develop to help you move forward?

- ❖ Situation:

- ❖ Lesson:

- ❖ Blessing:

- ❖ Recipe:

Chapter 20

Blessons: Happiness & Joy

Not too long ago, I noticed that a change was occurring in my life. Everything seemed to frustrate and drain me, from my business all the way down to my personal life. I took some time away from my business, people, and even little things which reminded me of work. Taking a moment to rest in a quiet place allowed me to hear that I was feeling so drained due to unhappiness. This feeling, served me with a reality check that I knew I had to face.

It is very often that we affiliate ourselves with things and call it happiness or joy, but when it runs low, we find ourselves back empty. I listened to my Pastor during one of his sermons regarding the distinction of joy. One thing he said that resonated with my spirit was that your joy is controlled by your priorities. Sometimes the things that bring you pleasure does not necessarily mean that it is joy. I then thought about the areas I felt joyful in and then it all made sense. My joy was identified through helping others, increasing clientele, because that meant bills were paid, and lastly, work. The things that so called brought me joy seemed to have now turned into burdens. There were fewer bookings due to the holiday season and the idea of how everything was going to work out financially just became overwhelming.

Through this process, I learned that if you put your trust in people, money, or anything else, it will fail you, but if you put your trust in God, He will lead the way. I then had to refill, reset, and reidentify myself, "Who is Christen?" Who is Christen without the letters behind her name? Who is Christen without the businesses? Who is Christen without the groups that she affiliates with? Who is Christen without the connections that she has? Who is Christen without the education? Who is Christen? With no time, I realized that I needed a break to reevaluate, revamp, and restructure my positioning and thinking in life.

After eliminating all of the extra noise, my focus was clear and had been filled; my joy didn't need to lie upon my business endeavors, but it needed to lie within. Just imagine yourself as an ATM machine that gives out money all of the time for free, but when someone actually takes the time to input a pin number to make a withdrawal, will your machine disburse anything if it is empty? Self-care is the ultimate best care and when we learn to do these things, we prioritize differently.

In this season of life, understanding that the direction of your joy matters is significant. It is not behind you, nor on the side of you, but instead, it lies before you. Joy is not a feeling; it is a focus.

"I have told you these things so that you will be filled with my joy. Yes, your joy will overflow!" (John 15:11 NLT)

- **My Lesson**: Learn to prioritize your focus.
- **My Blessing**: Learned the concept of becoming a healthier me
- **My Recipe**: Prioritize my focus in an area that reciprocates the same for me.

~JOURNAL MY BLESSON~

Think of a time when your happiness or joy was in the wrong place. What did you learn? How did your lesson serve as a blessing later in life? What recipe can you develop to help you move forward?

- ❖ Situation:

- ❖ Lesson:

- ❖ Blessing:

- ❖ Recipe:

Chapter 21

Blessons: All by Myself

As a young girl, I remember the days my mother used to read to me. I became more interested as she made it entertaining by her animated voices. There was one book in particular I enjoyed and it was called, *I Can Do It All by Myself*. After a few readings, I was then able to read the book all **by myself** at the age of three. This became my favorite book because I could simply do it all **by myself**.

Growing up, this mentality was kept. Although I displayed exceptional teamwork, there were just some things I preferred to do **by myself**. When it came to group work projects in school, I would often pull myself away from the group to work **by myself**. I seemed to always be paired with procrastinators, those that did not hold their end of the project and others that did not contribute anything. Why would I fail when I could do it all **by myself**?

The do it all by myself mentality took me far, but not as far in life. It was not until I began my first business that I would understand how hard it was to do things all **by myself**. I was excited to begin my business and was eager for it to be ran a certain way; therefore, I needed people that were aboard to be onboard. Once again, that did not happen for long. Some of my associates were only aboard to help me, but they were not onboard with showing up to meetings and contributing to the success of the organization, so it was in my best interest to let everyone go. Many of my associates volunteered not because they were passionate about what I was doing, but instead, they wanted to help me and they did the best they could but I needed consistency; so therefore, I chose to do it **by myself**.

As my associates went to pursue their own lives, I found myself afraid to network and ask anyone for their help because I thought that they would let me down, try and take my business away, take advantage of me, or even steal my ideas; so therefore, I did everything **by myself.** From grant writing, ordering products, promoting and advertising, maintaining paperwork, teaching, mentoring, coaching; yes, all of this was done **by myself**. Although I seemed to have mastered doing everything, I realized that I was tired of doing it all **by myself**.

Working on a project one day, I clearly heard God say that my business would not prosper with me running it alone. Although I knew I was capable of doing everything, I then thought how effective I would be if I were not burnt out and allowed others to help? This moment allowed me to realize how prideful I had become over a gift that was given to me and not essentially for me.

With great experience, it took me to learn that it is not within ourselves that we should seek our help from, but it is within the Lord above. All of our needs will be provided along with the right people at the right place and time. There will be a time where people will duplicate ideas, betray you, and leave you hanging, but it is within these times that it will help you learn and grow in character. Even if one person mistreats you, it does not mean that others will operate in the same way. The things that have worked for me were to have an open mind, maintain a sense of character, and of all, have a discerning spirit, because you may never know who will be used to help you prosper, but with hope and faith, you will learn that you **DO NOT HAVE TO DO IT BY YOURSELF.**

"So let us come boldly to the throne of our gracious God. There we will receive his mercy, and we will find grace to help us when we need it most." (Hebrews 4:16 NLT)

- **My Lesson**: It is impossible to do everything in our own strength, and some people will be specifically assigned to you to provide help.
- **My Blessing**: I have a network of people that are glad to help when I need it.
- **My Recipe**: When I am in need of help, I need to utilize the people that have been placed before me.

~JOURNAL MY BLESSON~

Think of a time when you needed help, but felt the need not to ask: What stopped you from asking and why? What did you learn? How did your lesson serve as a blessing later in life? What recipe can you develop to help you move forward?

- ❖ Situation:

- ❖ Lesson:

- ❖ Blessing:

- ❖ Recipe:

Chapter: 22

Blessons: Social Comparison

Have you ever compared yourself to others? You may be single and your friends are dating/married, or your friends may seem to have promising careers and you may not even know where your career even begins. If this is you, I just want to say do not get caught in the trap of social comparison. The social comparison theory is one that explains how individuals determine their social and personal worth based upon how they view others. The theory goes on to explain that we are in constant truth seeking of our own self-identity where we then compare ourselves to those around us to seek more clarity.

When we compare ourselves to others, we are either trying to do two things: self-evaluate, or self-enhance. To self-evaluate in the terms of social comparison is to compare oneself to a person to gain a better understanding of themselves and where they are presently in life. Self-enhancement is utilized when individuals compares themselves to someone else to boost up their level of confidence believing that there is nothing in common to compare.

Which trait can you identify yourself with? Self-evaluating, self-enhancing, or maybe even both? There have been times when I have experienced self-doubt, being overwhelmed, or even lonely that I began to self-evaluate as well as compare myself to those who were close to me. It is not that I ever was jealous of what my dear friends had, it was more of a, what about me moment. I would often ask myself if I was forgotten about when it came down to being married, having a family, wealthy, owning a successful business, and so much more? Although I may feel this way from time to time, I understand that my thoughts are not God's thoughts.

Have you ever experienced a time that you were doing something very important and just within a split second you found yourself scrolling on social media looking at everyone live their best life? One split second has now caused you an hour of time and possible feelings of uncertainty because you are not advancing as fast as someone else. This person may have not been exactly you, but it was me.

What I was doing wrong that things in my life would not manifest as fast as others? The answer to my question is focusing on the value of someone else's story. When we begin to compare ourselves to others, it becomes a never-ending spiral that leads to confusing thoughts about ourselves. For me, learning to grasp the concept of remaining humble and understanding that God is not in a rush to do anything provides me some hope within my process. My focus today is not trying to focus on what I do not specifically have but to celebrate what I do, because within the blink of an eye my time will come. **STAY READY!**

"Pay careful attention to your own work, for then you will get the satisfaction of a job well done, and you won't need to compare yourself to anyone else. For we are each responsible for our own conduct." (Galatians 6:4-5 NLT)

- **My Lesson**: Paying attention to others will not get you where you need to go any quicker.
- **My Blessing**: I have everything that I need in the season that I am in now.
- **My Recipe**: Turn off the extra noise in life and focus on yourself.

~JOURNAL MY BLESSON~

Think of a time when you compared yourself to someone. What type of feeling did that bring and why did you feel the need to do it? What did you learn? How did your lesson serve as a blessing later in life? What recipe can you develop to help you move forward?

- ❖ Situation:

- ❖ Lesson:

- ❖ Blessing:

- ❖ Recipe:

Chapter: 23

Blessons: Peace within the Fight

Have you ever been in a financial situation where it not only affected you, but it took a toll on your family's well-being? From the electricity being cut off, to no food on the table, to an eviction notice being served, are just a few of the toughest pills that anyone can swallow.

In the midst of situations that can seem so devastating and traumatizing, have you ever thought to respond with peace first? For those that can, you are my true inspiration and I applaud you and for those that find it difficult, I truly understand, because time after time you can be in a place of fear, worry, or being anxious about what will happen next. Why does it seem as if it is hard to find peace in the toughest times in our lives? My theory is because the condition of our mindset.

The condition of our mindset during periods of trials and tribulations can alter very quickly when we decide not to ask for assistance when needed. It is easy to develop the mindset that asking for help makes you weak, less of a responsible person, or that one day the kind action will later be used against you. For myself, I wanted to handle everything and not ask for help because I did not want to feel as if I were irresponsible or "needy." Truth is that we all hit hard times in our lives and if we have those that are in position to assist us then when should allow them to do so.

There was a time period in my life where I appeared to look great on the outside but was struggling on the inside. I smiled and kept pushing daily as I worked three positions five days a week just to pay my monthly bills. Overly consumed with work, I traveled from one position to another daily so that I did not have to ask for any financial help from anyone. I tried to maintain both my strength and composure, but that soon would break due to mental and physical exhaustion of working. After having a major meltdown, I got back up and decided to take control again to seek another paying position because I still did not want to ask for any help. I tried to make an extra position fit into my daily life schedule when I knew that I did not have the time, patience, nor interest and I just suddenly gave up.

The next day, I spoke to my sister and told her what was going on with me and it was her words that day that displayed the condition of my mindset. She said, "Christen, one of your main problems is that you think you have to be strong all of the time and not ask for help, you have sisters that can help you get through tough times. If I got it, you got it. We all win!" Tears then began to cloud my eyes because of all of what she said was true. I would probably have more peace in my life if I utilized my available resources. It is one thing to use and abuse resources, but it is another thing to turn back and be a resource to someone else. I then recognized that although I have physical resources, I did not even bother to use my spiritual resource as often as I should have because I felt that God knew my situation but yet he was not concerned.

I often thought that here I am trying to be less of the world, change for the greater good, pursue purpose, and yet, I am out here struggling, counting every penny just to make it! Is this supposed to be the rewarding feeling? A guest pastor from my church once said that it is one thing to make peace with God, but it is another thing to make peace with God daily. I made peace with God to commit to Him and try not to be of the world but I did not ever make a daily commitment. Each day will not always serve us the best dealt hand, but what is important is how we play the cards with the hand that was dealt. Although many days are filled with uncertainty, I have learned the best way to weather a storm is not to suffer in silence and ask for help if needed. Also point and pray in the direction that you need peace in.

If you are in collections because of medical bills, declare and decree them to be paid in full. Vacate the premises in 30 days; Declare and decree that the landlord will give an extended grace period. If you are homeless; Declare and decree that someone will grant you the opportunity to find work. I have learned and still learning that it is time to get what I have ordered and not settle or accept everything that has been sent. To have peace is to stand in confidence with the understanding that although everything is not perfect, you will overcome every step of the process.

"Don't worry about anything; instead, pray about everything. Tell God what you need, and thank him for all he has done. ⁷Then you will experience God's peace, which exceeds anything we can understand. His peace will guard your hearts and minds as you live in Christ Jesus." (Philippians 4:6-7 NLT)

- **My Lesson**: Do not lose your mind, nor heart in the move.
- **My Blessing**: I was reassured that I was never in a situation alone.
- **My Recipe**: Control what you can and pray about the rest.

~JOURNAL MY BLESSON~

Think of a time when you had a hard time finding peace in a situation. What are some of the tools you used to find it? What did you learn? How did your lesson serve as a blessing later in life? What recipe can you develop to help you move forward?

- ❖ Situation:

- ❖ Lesson:

- ❖ Blessing:

- ❖ Recipe:

Chapter: 24

Blessons: Push Season

Are you currently in a season where you feel as if you are pushing behind a car placed in neutral because it stalled on you? Or maybe you have placed a key in your ignition and although the lights on your panel come on, the vehicle does not turn over to start? Do you just sit in your feelings about where you are in your present moment, or do you take action and push?

From my personal experience, I find it easier coaching people to push than to actually apply the term for use for myself. Imagine telling a woman to push and birth a 10-pound baby, or telling a person running in a race to push harder because their opponent is right on their back; these moments become critical, and how you present yourself in the very moment of the process matters. With the woman in labor, it may take hours, but when the baby is ready, there is just no stopping.

Here it was at the top of the new year, I felt as if I was already five months in due to my process of enduring. From the feeling of struggling, overworking myself, not being where I wanted to be and a brand-new vehicle that suddenly stops working, was already enough on my plate. Many changes were made before the new year, especially involving the operations of my business. My business was temporarily placed on a hold simply because I noticed my focus was being redirected to operating into something greater.

My consulting side of business was very lucrative and I managed to always pay my bills and still have enough extra money to do anything that I wanted. Everything seemed to fall together, but I was shown that although it worked at a time of need, it did not mean it was my ultimate purpose and would work forever. I began to tune in to see exactly what I was supposed to be doing, and at this time it was different from consulting. Tuning in did not mean my bills would stop, nor did it make my life exempt from any circumstances; however, it honestly made me feel as if I wanted to revert back to what I knew and thought was best, which was to seek clients for consulting at a time when I was not supposed to. Oftentimes, I felt secure in my process because it seemed quick and easy, all I had to do was market myself every once in a while, and allow past clients to refer their friends and I had business but in reality, this was not exactly God's process.

While enduring a process that is not identified as your own, you will wait without knowing how long you will endure, there will be moments of silence, things will get tough, and you may shed some tears and want to throw in the towel and quit, but understand that anything worth fighting for is worth having. Just think how could I write a book on blessings if I have not gone through the process of learning lifelong lessons? How did Oprah Winfrey, Bill Gates, and Steve Jobs get to become wealthy billionaires? It is because they **PUSHED**. They pushed through trauma, abuse, low poverty, rejection, sickness, criticism, and so much more to get to where they are today. You are no different from them going out to do the same.

It is in our times of struggle, where we learn to activate our faith even when we cannot see the end result. I learned that your struggle may try and push you to revert to your old habits, but continue to be strong and to stand still. Time of endurance is where our greatest promises come from, so continue to move forward and PUSH (Pray until Something Happens) because your breakthrough is along the way.

"But as for you, be strong and courageous, for your work will be rewarded." (2 Chronicles 15:7 NLT)

- **My Lesson**: Following God's will for your life will not be easy.
- **My Blessing**: Through trials and tribulations, I am learning to not put trust within myself.
- **My Recipe**: Find hope in every situation, remain active, and push.

~JOURNAL MY BLESSON~

Think of a time when you chose to follow your own will. What happened? What did you learn? How did your lesson serve as a blessing later in life? What recipe can you develop to help you move forward?

- ❖ Situation:

- ❖ Lesson:

- ❖ Blessing:

- ❖ Recipe:

Chapter 25

Blessons: Faith Test

Do you ever use the excuse that you are waiting on a sign to make a big decision, move, or anything else in life? Well I do too, and I can agree that hearing clearly what my next move is supposed to be can be the most valued thing to do, but what happens when you do not get an answer but the only thing provided are bits and pieces? Do you stay in the unknown place until you fully get the clear to move, or do you move onto what has been shown or told to you?

The problem is that many of us have faith, but in the midst of being faithful, we also want certainty because it validates are faithfulness; however, faith does not operate as such. To have faith means to walk in confidence and to trust and believe in the things that are unseen. The entire plan for our lives will not be provided because if it were, we would not know how to exercise our faith. It is often in the unknown where you will find your greatest blessing, but in order for you to reach your purpose; you will be presented with a number of tests. Will you have faith and just move on the little bit that you have been shown, or will you continue to wait until the full blueprint is provided?

After hearing a sermon on faith, I began to realize that my pastor was talking to me. I had been faithful but yet stagnant all in the same time. Taking some time away from business to really ponder on how I would continue to operate left me stagnant. Instead of taking the little bit that I already knew, I chose to wait until I was shown a clearer picture, which did not get me anywhere. Operating as such, causes us to delay our blessing, and we often blame everything but ourselves when our blessings are held up.

Walking into the eyes of the uncertain can be fearful, especially when it has been told for you to do something that does not make sense to you, your family, or friends. Even when it does not make sense, you have to learn to take the leap of faith and do what you have been called to do in the season that you are in. Think of all the other times that you stepped out on faith. Did you fall? Even if you did, did you not get back up to try again? If you were told to do it, have faith that you will have the resources provided to bring you through it.

Nobody likes failure, or rejection, but we will never know what works until we push ourselves out there to just try. For me taking a leap of faith upon my calling was to begin a business, write a book, and even leave a fulltime job with benefits. Stepping out on faith requires a reason and sometimes it has nothing to do with you; but instead it is the beginning of your aligned purpose.

"Now someone may argue, "Some people have faith; others have good deeds." But I say, "How can you show me your faith if you don't have good deeds? I will show you my faith by my good deeds." (James 2:18 NLT)

- **My Lesson**: Having faith without action will get you nowhere.
- **My Blessing**: I am learning to put my confidence in my faith instead of certainty.
- **My Recipe**: If it came from God, He will not fall short on His Word.

~JOURNAL MY BLESSON~

What should you be actively doing in this season that you are in, and why aren't you doing it? What are you learning from your experience? How will your lesson serve as a blessing later in life? What recipe can you develop to help you move forward?

- ❖ Situation:

- ❖ Lesson:

- ❖ Blessing:

- ❖ Recipe:

Chapter 26

Blessons: Process of Purpose

Identifying or understanding your purpose can seem quite difficult when we are unable to see the bigger picture. You may find yourself walking in purpose, but then become distracted because of what others may say or think, you may lack resources for you to succeed, or maybe because of fear you have not moved. If any of these reasons apply to you, I want you to repeat after me three times, "I can have what I believe, if I believe it belongs to me."

It is so easy to quit and find something new because you no longer have to experience the blood, sweat, and tears behind something that you were working towards. Do not give up in this season that you are in because it is molding you to become the person you were called to be, whether that is a business owner, wife/husband, mother/father, mentor, speaker, or life coach: just know, you are called to be somebody greater.

The thought of purpose can seem like it is supposed to be a fulfillment to our own happiness at times, but in actuality, it is not. We have been designed for purpose to meet the needs of someone else. You may never know who is waiting on you to write the book as one person may have given up in the process of preparing theirs, someone may be waiting on your mission to begin a nonprofit so that your services can enhance their overall quality of life, or maybe an individual may be waiting for you to share your testimony because they are minutes away from contemplating suicide. You may never be able to answer the "why" and "how" of your purpose, but keep in mind to always answer when it calls.

A few weeks ago, I almost found myself giving up in purpose just because I felt that I hit rock bottom and the things that I was doing seemed to benefit others and not myself; therefore, I was willing to stop everything and enlist into the military. This was not a decision that I really wanted, but I felt like the journey in the military would take me faster in my process than working as an entrepreneur. My heart knew that this was wrong, but I forced my mind to believe that it was the right choice for me. The night after making a decision and contacting a recruiter, I had a dream about my military process that all went well until the day I had a medical exam. My medical exam determined that I was ineligible to continue along with the process because of something that was health related and that is when I woke up and was convinced that the military path was not the one for me.

What if I would have continued to pursue my thoughts of the military after I did or did not have the dream that I would be disqualified? I probably would have been highly upset to get so far along the process to only be rejected because of something I was not aware of. Where would this put me? Back in the same place I started, so at this point, I decided to make this entrepreneur life the best way possible, because an entrepreneur is a part of who I was called to become. The whole entire time I thought that I needed a change in career; but instead, I needed a change in my perspective.

How you view things can affect the way you will think, feel, and act. In this process, I learned to not become so consumed into what is and is not happening in life right now, because within the blink of an eye it could all change for the good or even the worse. Some of us will realize soon that you can no longer identify with certain jobs, people, or relationships because they are not purpose related. Purpose is not waiting nor is playing with any of us this year, and it is even more pressuring to hear that it will be by force or by choice to pursue it. Which one will you choose today?

"You can make many plans, but the Lord's purpose will prevail." (Proverbs 19:21 NLT)

- **My Lesson**: My purpose here on this earth will be identified by either force or by choice.
- **My Blessing**: I am operating much harder to make sure everything I choose in life is purpose related.
- **My Recipe**: When I cannot find myself in times of triumph, take a moment to realize how far I have come.

~JOURNAL MY BLESSON~

Think about a time in your life where you should have acted on purpose but you chose not to do so? What happened and what did you learn? How will your lesson serve as a blessing later in life? What recipe can you develop to help you move forward?

- ❖ Situation:

- ❖ Lesson:

- ❖ Blessing:

- ❖ Recipe:

Chapter 27

Blessons: Self Talk

What do you say to yourself when talking to yourself? It may sound like a bizarre question, but little do we know, our self-talk is one of the main influences of how we think, feel, and act. Our self-talk may include both our conscious and unconscious thoughts. The conscious mind refers to anything taking place within our current awareness such as memories, feelings, sensations, and perceptions while our unconscious mind normally stores fantasy and dreams, repressed memories of trauma, and serves as a sense of information processing. Things that we do not want our conscious mind to be aware of, we tend to allow it to slip into the unconscious mind.

Your success or failure with anything will depend on your overall programming. Just think of what kind of day you will start off with if you spoke positive affirmations to yourself? There is so much power in the words that you speak, especially when using, "I AM." You are what you say you are, so if you are great, believe you are great, if you are successful, believe you are successful. Life and death begin within the power of your tongue.

I am _____
I am _____
I am _____

When you are able to confess and declare what you are and who you are, there is nothing that should be able to stop you from becoming what you have said, unless you allow it. When you allow your circumstances and situations in life to change your outcome of your self-talk, it begins to alter your cognition and what once was, I am then becomes I am not. Having the I am not voice within can serve as the loudest voice you hear. This voice can become so loud that it begins to affect your feelings and actions.

In order to keep us from getting to this place, we must learn how to give these negative thoughts a name and send them back to where they came from. When I failed my licensing counseling exam, I associated myself as being a failure and I felt like I was not worthy to even use the term therapist, although I was certified. I lost confidence in myself at a point in time allowing the failure to define who I was rather than changing my perception and focusing on who I was called to become.

When I experience periods of fear, anxiety, or depression, I name it all in one cluster as self-doubt, and command and decree that it has no place in my space. I not only have to command and declare this affirmation, but with it I have to believe that this is so. It would be quite challenging for any of us to speak these things about our lives if we did not sincerely believe it. The challenge is not in who you are, but it is in who you have been called to be.

"But whatever I am now, it is all because God poured out his special favor on me--and not without results. For I have worked harder than any of the other apostles; yet it was not I but God who was working through me by his grace."
(1 Corinthians 15:10 NLT)

- **My Lesson**: I have learned how my thoughts of who I say I am can have a deep effect on what I become.
- **My Blessing**: I am learning to speak great things despite my circumstances each day.
- **My Recipe**: Speak life in all of your situations.

~JOURNAL MY BLESSON~

Think of a time when your negative thoughts about yourself took over your life. What happened, and what did you do to change your faulty thinking? What did you learn? How will your lesson serve as a blessing later in life? What recipe can you develop to help you move forward?

- ❖ Situation:

- ❖ Lesson:

- ❖ Blessing:

- ❖ Recipe

Chapter 28

Blessons: Are you Grateful?

What does it truly mean to be grateful? You may associate the term with being thankful, expressing gratitude, having a great attitude, or everlasting joy. In life, we find ourselves grateful for a lot of things such as our house, car, food, and even our jobs because these things serve as our immediate needs, but what about the other little things that we should be grateful for?

Waking up another morning in your right mind, having the opportunity to have a job you may not like to produce income, or just even cherishing another day being alive, although you may be diagnosed with cancer. These are the few moments that sometimes we can take for granted because of the act of being caught in our own circumstances and bypassing the promise.

Both your breakthrough and your promise will lie in a place where your eyes will be unable to see, your mind will not understand, and your heart may grow weary, but in times of trials and tribulations, we must learn to remain humble and grateful within the circumstances that we are presented with. Being grateful is not the easiest concept to apply in all situations because it can become hard to see the good out of everything that seems to be going wrong or not going the way that you intended.

Due to our own expectations about life, we tend to have the mindset of solving our problems on the level of our own understanding, but what if I told you that there is someone that exceeds your own understanding and expectation and makes a way through your good days and bad would you believe me?

There was a time in my life where I remember working a few positions temporarily during a week and in one position they only gave me three hours to work. I was very adamant of not going in because I felt that working three hours was a waste of my time and gas, so I decided not to go with the intentions of attending a class that was technically already "sold out" for business. The days of this season made me feel as if I were in survival mode, which meant that I had to do what I had to do to pay my bills, even if it meant operating three different side hustles while pursuing my own business. This desperate place in life had me miss the concept and purpose in a lot of things because there was so much emphasis that I placed in the monetary value and how to get it.

I did not want to go to work, because in my eyes it was only $27 minus tax that I would be earning for that day, and I could not wrap my mind around that even though it would have been more than I would have made if I had not gone. Mentioning my thought process to someone of wise counsel, then told me that I was so caught up with the monetary value of just receiving $27 that I may be missing the actual purpose of that particular day. Also mentioning that I could be in the right place at the right time to save someone, or how someone could be specifically looking for me to provide counseling, coaching, and consulting service with their next big idea, but I would never know if I did not show up.

I began to think about all of this, and although I wanted to be imprisoned within my own mindset of earning $27, I knew my heart was telling me otherwise. Although, I could not see within my own two eyes, wrap my mind around it, or even obtain the value of the experience at the present moment, I knew that if my mindset would switch to just be grateful for the three hours of work, than I would be blessed with an opportunity, and that day I most certainly was.

"If you are faithful in little things, you will be faithful in large ones. But if you are dishonest in little things, you won't be honest with greater responsibilities"
(Luke 16:10 NLT)

- **My Lesson**: God will meet all of our needs not our level of expectations for our lives.
- **My Blessing**: I am learning how to humble myself and find gratefulness in all situations that I encounter.
- **My Recipe**: In the moments you feel like quitting, know that this is normally a moment before a miracle happens. Do not give up!

~JOURNAL MY BLESSON~

Think of a time that you were ungrateful in your present situation. What happened and what did you learn? How will your lesson serve as a blessing later in life? What recipe can you develop to help you move forward?

- ❖ Situation:

- ❖ Lesson:

- ❖ Blessing:

- ❖ Recipe:

Chapter 29

Blessons: Dark Places

Take a moment and think about some places that we consider dark? An ally may come to mind, or even a dark room to develop pictures, but what about those dark places in our own lives? You know, the dark place of losing a loved one, the ending of a long-term relationship, the struggle to put food on the table, or even the tough days of raising a child as a single parent. These are only some of the examples that many may go through that eventually lead them into a dark place of anger, depression, doubt, bitterness, hurt, or rage, but what if I told you that being in the dark can be turned into something greater!

There was once a time in my life where I felt that I was in a dark place. It seemed as if everything around me was crashing, people I loved the most were hurting me, and I developed a sense of hatred that became deeply rooted within. I realized I lost my joy and I was digging myself into a black hole of depression and bitterness, and there was no way that I could see the positive in the situation, so I sought out counseling. Counseling allowed me to not only work through what I was feeling, but it allowed me to change my thought patterns and reactions towards certain situations that seemed to trigger me. Committing myself to this process, has allowed me to become a greater person in all areas of life.

Think about how pictures were developed in the 19th century before Polaroid cameras. Photos were developed in a dark room with a projector in which helped project light to an image of negative base which controls the focus to develop images. Once the sheet of photography paper that served as the negative is exposed to the light, it turns into a positive image.

So now let's break this process down a little more. Imagine yourself as the image of a negative base that is waiting to be developed in a dark room. In the dark room you are alone and experiencing signs of negativity, heartbreak, grief, and denial. Do you just sit there in misery of these things that are occurring, or do you find the projecting light within your circumstances? Speaking life into your situation, praying, meditating, reading, or singing a joyful tune are all examples of projectors that shed light and controls your focus on developing a positive image. Once the image is exposed to the proper amount of light, it then turns from a negative into a positive.

Dark places in our lives can make us feel very empty on the inside, but understand the things that you are experiencing has nothing to do with you, it is for someone else. It does not make sense to you, but in reality, it does not have to make sense. Obedience has prompted me for position and allowed me to see that it is in dark places where you will stumble upon your greatest blessings. Breakthrough is about breaking the individual, because there is an ultimate purpose behind the pain.

"Jesus spoke to the people once more and said, "I am the light of the world. If you follow me, you won't have to walk in darkness, because you will have the light that leads to life." (John 8:12 NLT)

- **My Lesson**: Sometimes we do not have the power to control dark spaces in life and we need help from others.
- **My Blessing**: I was able to recognize how my dark place in life was really taking a toll upon me, and I sought help
- **My Recipe**: When you feel that you are in a dark space, understand that it is a transitional phase, embrace it, and seek resources that will help you through the process

~JOURNAL MY BLESSON~

Think of a time when you found yourself in a dark place. What happened and what did you do to get out of that place? What did you learn? How will your lesson serve as a blessing later in life? What recipe can you develop to help you move forward?

- ❖ Situation:

- ❖ Lesson:

- ❖ Blessing:

- ❖ Recipe:

Chapter 30

Blessons: Trust

We all at one point of time in our lives put our trust in the wrong things. Becoming an entrepreneur has *been rewarding, but it has been tough. One of the questions that an entrepreneur may ask daily is: How will I make enough money to pay for everything that I have?* This was my question to myself many days, but I have never been put into the position where I had to actually fully trust God, until now.

Excited to jump into entrepreneurship seemed great, enough money was saved up for a few months' rent, car was paid off, and bills were pretty low because it was just me living alone, but I always knew that as long as I was enrolled in school that in the fourth week, I would receive a nice refund check that I could survive off of. You may now want to ask if I put my trust in a refund check and to answer, yes, I did because I knew that I would be covered. Life was great when I had refund checks and would only have to substitute teach for a few days out of the week and work on my business, but then I graduated once again. As exciting as this day was, it was actually the day when my life began to change. I put my trust in a refund check, and now it was gone. *Now what was next?* Back to the drawing board of pulling more days of substitute teaching, but also realizing my credit score is the highest it's ever been, so I then began to put my trust in credit cards to pay for things that I needed. The way I broke down paying my bills were to make payments on the credit cards with cash and then use the credit cards to pay other bills. Living as such for five years is clearly not the standard way of living, but it worked for me until the day every single credit card that I owned was maxed.

My credit score began to drop because of the heavy usage, and I could no longer put my faith in credit cards, so I began to put my faith in clients with my business. Although majority of my clients never cancelled on me, I did have some clients that did because life happens to all of us. The process of my thinking was out of order and one day I became very frustrated with my finances and was then brought back to all of these scenarios. My trust was put in a refund check, credit cards, and people to supply my needs, but when all these things depleted, I felt lost and had absolutely nothing.

I was allowed to go through the process of being comfortable of knowing for a couple of seasons to only now experience the wilderness with dark shades on. There are many days that I feel that I do not know where I am going and saying yes to God when there is no tracing can be quite tough but through this experience, I realize that there is funk in the process of not knowing, and it will stink, but to have the understanding that there are some things in experience that can only be taught while enduring the process is priceless.

"Jesus spoke to the people once more and said, "I am the light of the world. If you follow me, you won't have to walk in darkness, because you will have the light that leads to life." (John 8:12 NLT)

- **My Lesson**: You have the power to maneuver through your dark spaces in life.

- **My Blessing**: I was able to recognize how my dark place in life was really taking a toll upon me and I sought help.
- **My Recipe**: When you feel that you are in a dark space, understand that it is a transitional phase, learn to embrace it, and seek resources that will help you through the process

~JOURNAL MY BLESSON~

Think of a time when you had to put your trust in something greater than yourself. What happened and how did it make you feel? What did you learn? How will your lesson serve as a blessing later in life? What recipe can you develop to help you move forward?

- ❖ Situation:

- ❖ Lesson:

- ❖ Blessing:

- ❖ Recipe:

Chapter 31

Blessons: Birthing

I can only imagine how much pain that is involved in the childbearing process. From the time it takes for a child to formulate, the stretching of your body, laboring pains, and of all, remaining patient in the process enduring childbirth can leave emotions on an ultimate high and low. One moment you find yourself happy, and the next moment you find yourself tired or in pain, but do you quit pushing your greatest creation into the world? No, you don't! You keep pushing until you hear the first cry of your newborn child.

Childbirth is very similar to birthing a business or pursing purpose. There are good days and then there are not so good days. When is the last time you really remember going through growing pains? I can only imagine that it hurt, caused some anxiety and depression, and it may have put you in a place that you just wanted to give up, but did you? My response is, if you have gotten this far into reading this book, then you have pressed your way.

The days of morning sickness and roller coaster emotions are going to come, whether you are pregnant with child or not, but the ultimate key is to look beyond where you are and look to the days that are coming. When a child is growing in its mother's womb, her belly expands, but when the water breaks, it is just a matter of time that the blessing will be revealed.

Are you here in life? Carrying a baby on the inside waiting for its birth date? On three different occasions this has been my story. I knew that I wasn't pregnant with child but I saw images of me carrying something in my belly. The first time I dreamed, I saw myself pregnant, cute, and round. The second dream, my belly expanding, and just recently, my last dream consisted of me being in labor lying on my side preparing to have whatever it was I was carrying. Waking up from this fascinating dream allowed me to become very anxious of knowing what was next. As I calmed down to seek clarity of what I had seen, I was able to understand that the process of the desires of my heart were on its way.

Enduring the process for myself consisted of being mentally, physically, spiritually, and emotionally enabled, developed, pruned, and having the ability to go through laboring pains that helped strengthen the muscle that I needed for the current season that I am in. I have grown to understand that there will be many routine slow days, but if I remain consistent in who I am and who I have been called to be that my life will begin to manifest. Patience is the process that will prevent you from miscarrying your promise.

"The time will come," says the LORD, "when the grain and grapes will grow faster than they can be harvested. Then the terraced vineyards on the hills of Israel will drip with sweet wine! I will bring my exiled people of Israel back from distant lands, and they will rebuild their ruined cities and live in them again. They will plant vineyards and gardens; they will eat their crops and drink their wine. I will firmly plant them there in their own land. They will never again be uprooted from the land I have given them," says the LORD your God." (Amos 9:13-15 NLT)

- **My Lesson**: In order to get to your promise, you will have to endure the process.
- **My Blessing**: I am beginning to bear fruit in the season that I am in because of my fight in the process.
- **My Recipe**: Before taking on anything extra, learn to master what is present within your hands.

~JOURNAL MY BLESSON~

Think of your own laboring experience with giving birth to a child or new idea. What happened and what did you do to change your faulty thinking? What did you learn? How will your lesson serve as a blessing later in life? What recipe can you develop to help you move forward?

- ❖ Situation:

- ❖ Lesson:

- ❖ Blessing:

- ❖ Recipe:

THIRTY-WON

This is most certainly the year of Thirty-Won Blessons. How does it feel? If I have successfully done my part in preparing you for the reading of this entire book, then you should not only have your own 31 Blessons, but you should now be able to write a new narrative. Allow me to reintroduce myself: My name is_____

_____
_____
_____
_____
_____
_____
_____
_____
_____
_____
_____
_____
_____
_____
_____
_____
_____
_____
_____
_____

To be continued……

About the Author

Christen Miller, MAHS, MA

From a Military Brat, to 8 1/2 years of higher education faced with trials and tribulations, to stepping out on faith and leaving her 9-5 job to become an entrepreneur is just a glimpse of the 31 years of her life. Today Ms. Miller serves as a renowned philanthropist, entrepreneur, therapist, life coach, nonprofit consultant, educator, and so much more! Over the years, she has learned to create a lane of her own and develop recipes that have led to her future success, thus far. With her new book, *31 Blessons,* she hopes to aspire to inspire you to do the same.

"I have 31 Blessons and so do you! I Teach, You Learn…Going Global!" ~Ms. Miller~

Blessons Business Sponsors

Bella Hearts, Inc
Nonprofit Organization
Greensboro, NC
336-814-7747
Bellasheartsfab5@gmail.com
Instagram-Bellaheartsfab5
Facebook- Bella Hearts, Inc.

Carolina Chicken and Waffles
Greenville, NC
252-258-3562
Linktr.ee/carolinachickenwafles
Instagram- Carolinachickenwaffles
Facebook- Carolina Chicken & Waffles

Cato Kelly
Leesay Allure Beauty Supply
Biscoe, NC
910-828-4078 (store)
910-975-5493 (cell)
www.LeesayAllure.com
Instagram-Leesayallure
Facebook- Leesay Allure Beauty Supply

Crystal Shepperd
Crystal Lips (Lipstick and Lip Gloss)
Fayetteville, NC
910-583-6783
Cshephe5@eagles.nccu.edu
Instagram- Crystallips4ever
Facebook- Crystallips4ever

Dark Red Photography
Fayetteville, NC
910-638-7557
Darkredphotography@gmail.com
www.darkredphotography.com
Instagram- Darkred_photography
Facebook- DARKRED Photography

Dr. Jalaal Hayes
Elyte Universal Network
Wilmington, Delaware
484-380-5280
info@elyteunetwork.com
Instagram-Elyteunetwork
Facebook- Elyte Universal Network

Future Endeavors Life Program
Nonprofit Organization
Fayetteville, NC
910-527-9231
www.futureendeavorslp.org
Instagram- Futureendeavorslp
Facebook- Future Endeavors Life Program

Hope and Vision Outreach
Nonprofit Consulting, Coaching, and Counseling
Burlington, NC
www.hopeandvisionoutreach.com
Instagram- Hopeandvisionoutreach
Facebook- Hope and Vision Outreach

Kurin Keys
822-Tees, Inc.
Fayetteville, NC
910-822-8337
www.822tees.com
Instagram- 822Tees
Facebook- 822Tees

Keisha Thompson
Sophisticated Jewels by KT
Paparazzi Accessories
Burlington, NC
336-512-2532
Krthomps@yahoo.com
Paparazziaccessories.com/253941

La'Donya Benning
Her Crafts
Junction City, Kansas
910-248-9245
Hercrafts.bigcartel.com
Facebook- Her Crafts

Making Visions
Nonprofit/Home Health
Agency/CNA School
Burlington/Fayetteville, NC
336-222-9797/910-485-7505
makingvisions@aol.com

Nariahs Way Foundation
Nonprofit Organization
Asheboro, NC
910-220-9940
www.nariahswayfoundation.org
Instagram-Nariahsway
Facebook- Nariahs Way Foundation

Phyllis Sneed
Atomi
Fayetteville, NC
910-583-7948
Savvy9000@aol.com
www.usaatomy.com
Facebook- Phyllis Sneed

Samod Wilson
Painting on Purpose
Fayetteville, NC
www.samodwilson.com
Instagram- Paintingonpurpose
Facebook- Painting on Purpose

Shireen Campbell
Inclusively 4 U Apparel and Accessories
Fayetteville, NC
Inclusively4u@gmail.com
www,inclusively4u.com
Facebook- Inclusively4U
Instagram- Inclusively4U

Shakeema Saloane
Operation Credit, LLC
Fayetteville, NC
910-863-1822
contact@opscredit.com

Tammy "TAZ Z"
Rock the Tazbah Photography
Zebulon, NC
919-904-2999
Instagram- Rockthetazbahphotography
Facebook Rockthetazbahphotography

Tenisha Dunlap
Trust and Believe Photography
Asheboro, NC
910-220-9940
trustandbelievephotography.com
Instagram- Trustandbelievephotoraphy
Facebook- Trust and Believe Photography

Visions of Hope Therapeutic Services PLLC
Behavioral Health Counseling
Burlington/Fayetteville NC
336-222-9797/910-485-7505

Winks N Blinks
Cosmetology/Lashes/Lash Trainer
Burlington, NC
336-639-9911 (Text)
winksnblink@gmail.com
Instagram- WinksnBlink
Facebook- Winks N Blink

Follow Us

Instagram- 31blessons

Facebook- Circle of Blessons

Listen to our *31 Blessons...Heyyy Sis* Podcast on Spotify, Apple Podcast, Anchor, and Overcast

Counseling Hotlines

Substance Abuse Disorders

- Al-Anon Family Groups (888) 425-2666
- National Council on Alcoholism and Drug Dependence (800) 622-2255
- Narcotics Anonymous (866) 624-35780
- SAMHSA: National Helpline (800) 662-4357

Suicide and Crisis

- Crisis Call Center (775) 784-8090 or text ANSWER to 839863
- Depression Hotline (630) 482-9696
- Disaster Distress Helpline (800) 985-5990 or text Talk with Us to 66746
- National Suicide Prevention Lifeline (800) 273-8255

Domestic and Sexual Violence Hotline/Child Abuse

- Domestic Violence Hotline/Child Abuse (800) 799-7233
- Elder Abuse Hotlines (800) 252-8966
- National Domestic Violence Hotline (800)799-7233
- Rape, Abuse, Incest, National Network (RAINN) (800) 656-HOPE (4673)
- Sexual Abuse - Stop It Now! (888) PREVENT (7738368)

Eating Disorders

- National Association of Anorexia Nervosa and Eating Disorders (630) 577-1330
- National Eating Disorder Referral and Information Center (858) 481-1515
- National Eating Disorders Association (800) 931-2237

Gay & Lesbian National / GLBTQ

- Gay & Lesbian National Hotline (888)843-4564 or text ANSWER to 839863
- Gay & Lesbian Trevor HelpLine Suicide Prevention (800) 850-8078
- Gay Men's Domestic Violence Program (800) 832-1901
- GLBT National Youth Talkline (800) 246-PRIDE (77433)
- Trans Lifeline (877) 565-8860

Specific Disorders / Other

- National Institute of Mental Health Information Center (866) 615-6464
- National Victims of Crime Center 1 (800) FYI-CALL (1-800-394-2255)
- Tragedy Assistance Program for Survivors (TAPS) (800) 959-8277
- American Chronic Pain Association (800)-533-3231
- CHADD-Children & Adults with Attention Deficit/Hyperactivity Disorder (800) 233-4050
- Depression and Bipolar Support Alliance (DBSA) (800) 826-3632

- Grief Recovery Institute (818) 907-9600
- Harvard Eating Disorders Center (888) 236-1188
- National Center for Learning Disabilities (NCLD) (888) 575-7373
- National Alliance on Mental Illness (NAMI) (800) 950-NAMI (6264)
- Panic Disorder Information Hotline 800- 64-PANIC (72642)

Sexual Health / Pregnancy

- AIDS Hotline (Youth only) (800) 788-1234
- AIDS National Hotline (800)-342-2437
- AIDS info (800) 448-0440
- American Pregnancy Helpline (866) 942-6466
- American Sexual Health Association (919) 361-8488
- Baby Safe Haven (888) 510-2229
- National AIDS Hotline (800) 232-4636
- Planned Parenthood National Hotline (800) 230-7526
- Postpartum Support International (800) 944-4773
- Project Inform HIV/AIDS Treatment Hotline (800) 822-7422
- PAR (People Against Rape) (843) 745-0144
- STD Hotline (800) 227-8922

Youth and Parenting

- Adolescent Crisis Intervention & Counseling Nineline (800) 999-9999
- Child at Risk Hotline (800) 792-5200
- Child Welfare Information Gateway (800)-FYI-3366 (800-394-3366)

- Child Welfare Information Gateway (800)-FYI-3366 (800-394-3366)
- Childhelp National Child Abuse Hotline 800-4-A-CHILD (800 4-2-24453
- CyberTipline for reporting the exploitation of children (800)-843-5678
- Missing & Exploited Children Hotline (800)-843-5678
- National Center for Missing & Exploited Children Hotline 1-800-THE-LOST (1-800-843-5678)
- National Runaway Switchboard (800) 786-2929
- Parental Stress Line (800) 632-8188
- Speak Up Prevent Gun Violence (866) 773-2587
- Teen Helpline (800) 400-0900
- Thursday's Child National Youth Advocacy Hotline (800) 872-5437

References

BibleGateway

https://www.biblegateway.com

Free Telephone Counseling Hotlines in the US

https://www.opencounseling.com/hotlines-us

The Bible App

https://www.youversion.com/the-bible-app

www.ingramcontent.com/pod-product-compliance
Lightning Source LLC
Chambersburg PA
CBHW030901170426
43193CB00009BA/695